WINTER CONSTELLATIONS

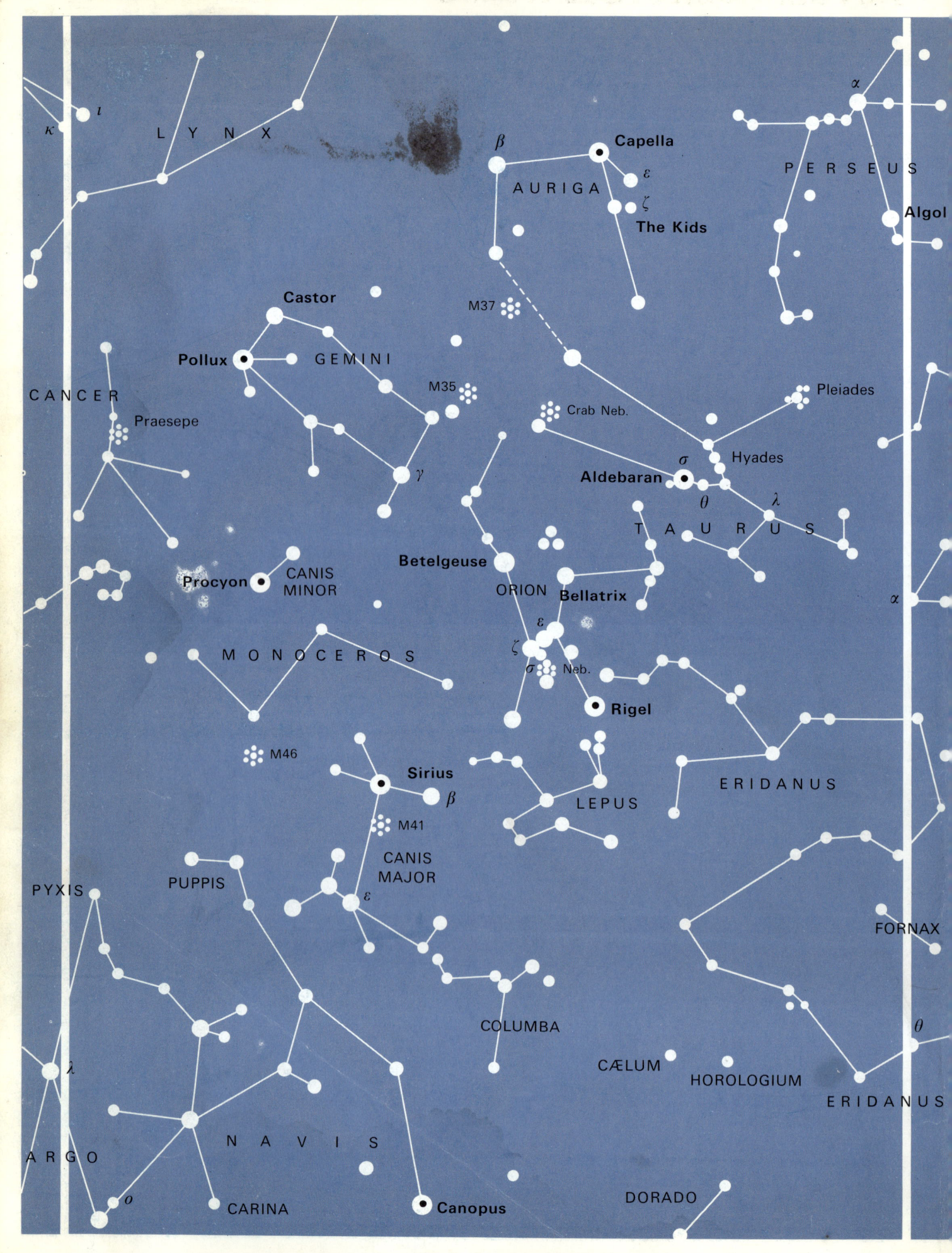

AUTUMN CONSTELLATIONS

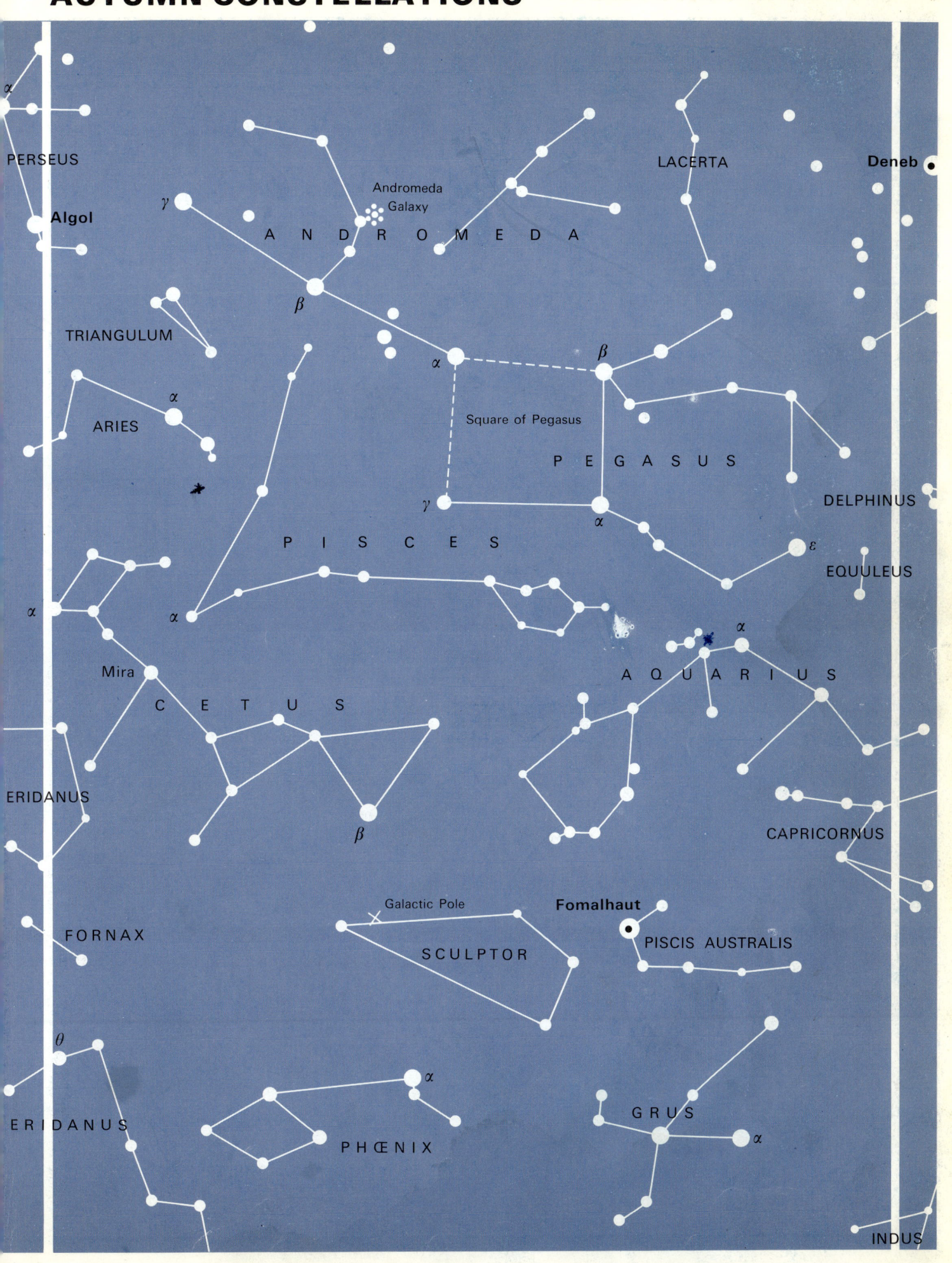

PERSEUS

Algol

α

γ

TRIANGULUM

ARIES

α

Andromeda
Galaxy

A N D R O M E D A

β

α

Square of Pegasus

LACERTA

Deneb

β

P E G A S U S

DELPHINUS

γ

α

P I S C E S

ε

EQUULEUS

α

α

Mira

C E T U S

A Q U A R I U S

α

ERIDANUS

β

CAPRICORNUS

FORNAX

Galactic Pole

SCULPTOR

Fomalhaut

PISCIS AUSTRALIS

θ

E R I D A N U S

α

PHŒNIX

G R U S

α

INDUS

Adventures with Astronomy

Percy Seymour

John Murray

'To Dianna'

Acknowledgements

The author wishes to thank the following for their help:

Mr G. S. Pearce and Mr R. Stewart for help and advice; the RAS Librarian for supplying photographs from the collection; Mr G. Y. Haig for allowing me to describe the Scotch mount designed by him; those people who have allowed me to use their photographs as stated below; and my wife, for her help in producing the manuscript.

Photographs: 2 (Polish Cultural Institute, London); 4a, 4b, 5, 17.2, 20.3, 20.4, 20.5, 21.1 (Hale Observatories); 15.4a (C. C. Hall); 15.4b (C. Hunt); 16.1, 21.2 (Lick Observatory); 19.21 (William Day Planetarium); 21.3 (W. J. S. Lockyer, Sidmouth 1922: Royal Astronomical Society Photographic Collection); 21.4 (H. G. Miles); 21.19 (Clive Purchase, Plymouth Astronomical Society).

Star charts: Grateful acknowledgement is due to George Philip and Son Ltd for permission to base the star charts on p. 21 and the endpapers on *Philip's Chart of the Stars*.

© Percy Seymour 1983

First published 1983
by John Murray (Publishers) Ltd
50 Albemarle Street, London W1X 4BD

Printed in Great Britain by
Richard Clay (The Chaucer Press) Ltd, Bungay, Suffolk
Filmset in Monophoto Plantin by
Northumberland Press Ltd, Gateshead

British Library Cataloguing in Publication Data

Seymour, Percy
    Adventures with astronomy.
    1. Astronomy
    I. Title
    520   QB45

ISBN 0-7195-3945-5
ISBN 0-7195-3931-5 Pbk

CONTENTS

Astronomy – the oldest science

Astronomy was studied in the ancient world, long before any other sciences like physics, chemistry or medicine. Why were people interested in watching the stars when there were urgent things to do here on Earth? Surely it was more important to be well fed, to keep warm and to protect oneself against wild animals? People in these early times depended for food either on hunting or on gathering food from trees and plants. They knew that animals, birds and plants were not available all the time, but they had no calendar, as we have today, to help them plan their hunting and gathering to coincide with times when food was available. However, they soon realised that the night sky was constantly changing with the seasons of the year. The star maps associated with Project 9 will show you this.

These early hunter–gatherers must have noticed, for example, that when certain patterns of stars were on the eastern horizon immediately after sunset, it was always at the time of year when certain berries were ripe for eating. They may also have noticed that some birds and animals would disappear from the landscape for a period, only to reappear when other patterns of stars were appearing on the eastern horizon after sunset. In this way they developed the use of the sky as a calendar, and when eventually these very early peoples settled down as farmers, they used this sky calendar to help them decide when to sow seeds and prepare for the following seasons. This calendar is still with us, the star patterns changing slightly night after night throughout the year, as they have done for centuries.

Ancient astronomers also used the Sun to tell time during the day and the stars to tell time during the night. Also, we know from the way they built their temples and pyramids that they could find direction from the stars and the Sun.

Making calendars, telling time of day and direction-finding were the important tasks of the ancient astronomers. For our present knowledge of the Earth, stars and planets we owe a great deal to the early skywatchers.

All early observations were made without the use of telescopes. These naked-eye discoveries could give very little information on the distance to the Sun, the Moon and the stars, so there were many different ideas about how such bodies were arranged in space. One idea was that all the stars were attached to the inside of a very large sphere surrounding our Earth, which was in the centre. Ancient astronomers also discovered that there were some strange stars that wandered about between the other stars. These 'wanderers' we now call the *planets*. It was thought that each of the five planets that could be seen with the naked eye was attached to a transparent sphere of its own. The universe was thus thought to be a series of transparent balls with the Earth at the centre, with each ball containing one object and the outermost ball containing all the so-called *'fixed'* stars – i.e. those which appear not to move in relation to each other. Although we no longer look at the universe in this way, this idea was considered to be right for hundreds of years and in its time provided a useful model from which all sorts of discoveries were made.

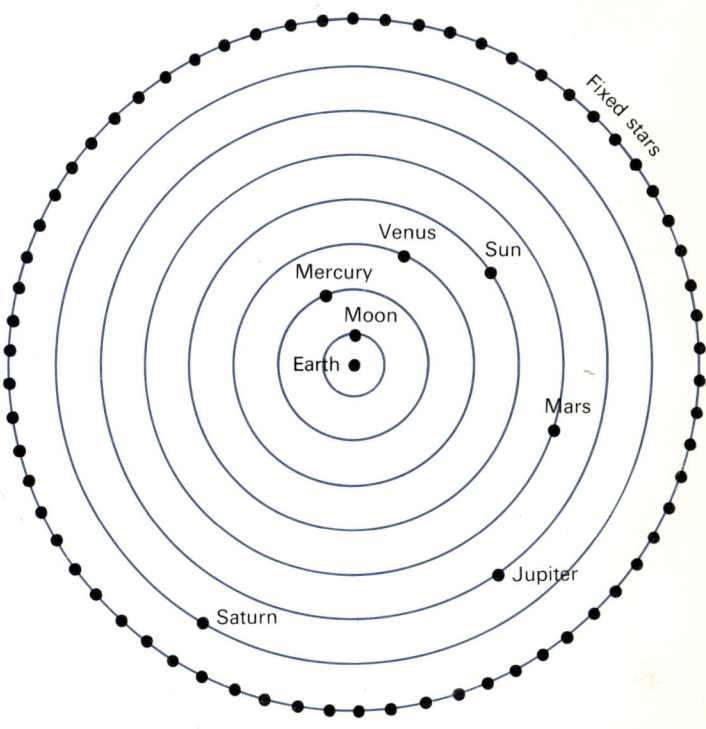

Fig. 1 An ancient view of the universe

The work of men like Copernicus, Tycho Brahe, Galileo and Newton, and the invention of the telescope, led to our present view of the Solar System. This is simply the little group of bodies, including the Earth, that surrounds our Sun. We now know that there are nine major planets going round the Sun in paths that are not quite circles, but slightly distorted circles called *ellipses*. Some of the planets show phases like our Moon, and several planets have moons of their own. Also going round the Sun are a large number of much smaller planets called asteroids, swarms of solid particles, rocks and stones called meteor showers, and large snowballs with long tails of vapour called comets.

Our Sun is a star, quite ordinary and like countless others, but it is so close to Earth that we see it as a hot ball in the sky rather than just a point of light. Studies made by telescope in many parts of the world have shown that most stars are very large, hot spheres of gas and many are much bigger than our own Sun. Some of them occur singly, others occur in groups of two or more, and some occur in large clusters of stars. The distances to the stars are so great that they are measured in light years, one light year being the distance travelled by a beam of light in

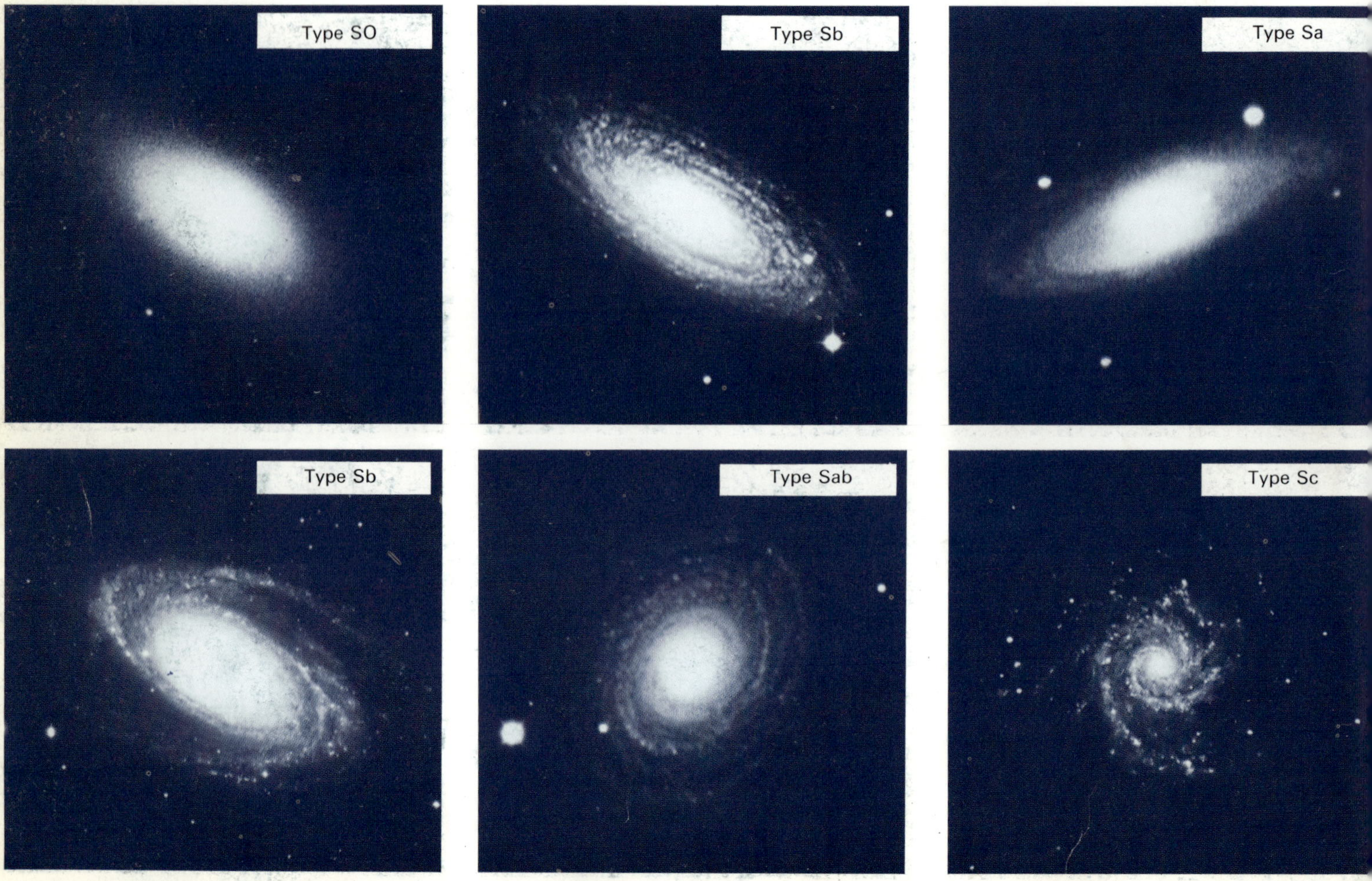

Fig. 2 Nicolas Copernicus, 1473–1543, gave us our present view of the Solar System

Type SO

Type Sb

Type Sa

Type Sb

Type Sab

Type Sc

Fig. 4 Different types of galaxies: **(a)** Normal spiral galaxies

Mercury
Sun
Venus
Earth
Jupiter
Mars
Saturn
Pluto
Uranus
Neptune

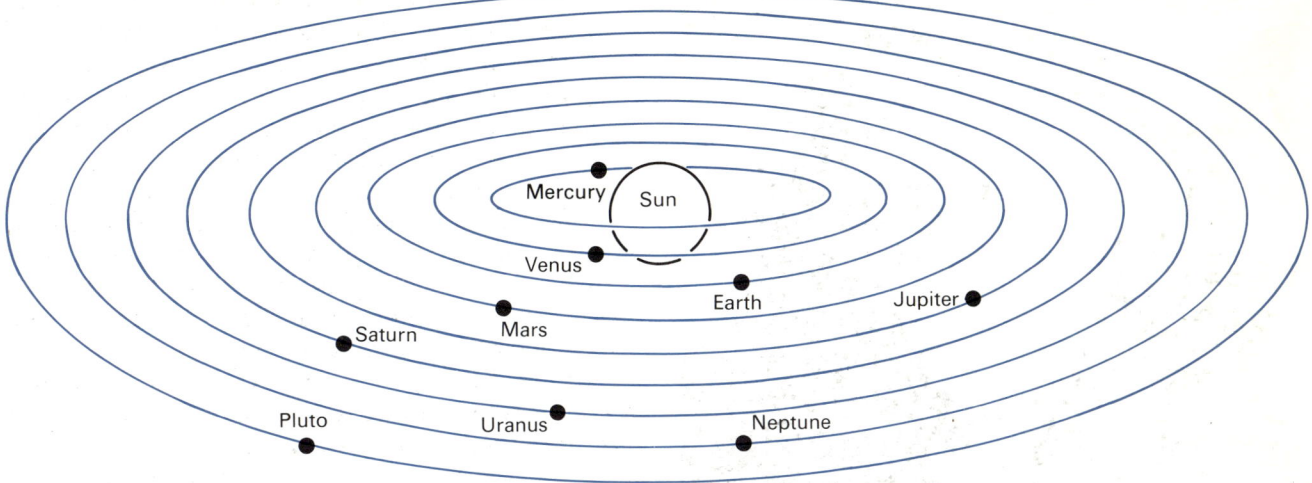

Fig. 3 A modern view of the Solar System

one year, or about ten million million kilometres.

Look upwards on a very clear night somewhere far away from city lights, and you may see a beautiful, hazy band of light stretching across the sky; this is the Milky Way. Discoveries made with telescopes tell us that it consists of 100 000 000 000 stars. Some of these stars are to be found within large clouds of gas, but there are also gas and dust clouds between the stars. Our Milky Way is like a city of stars with a city centre called the nucleus and spiral highways leading from the city centre. Our Sun is one of the many stars along one highway, about two thirds out towards the edge of the city.

In the early part of this century large telescopes in America showed many other galaxies

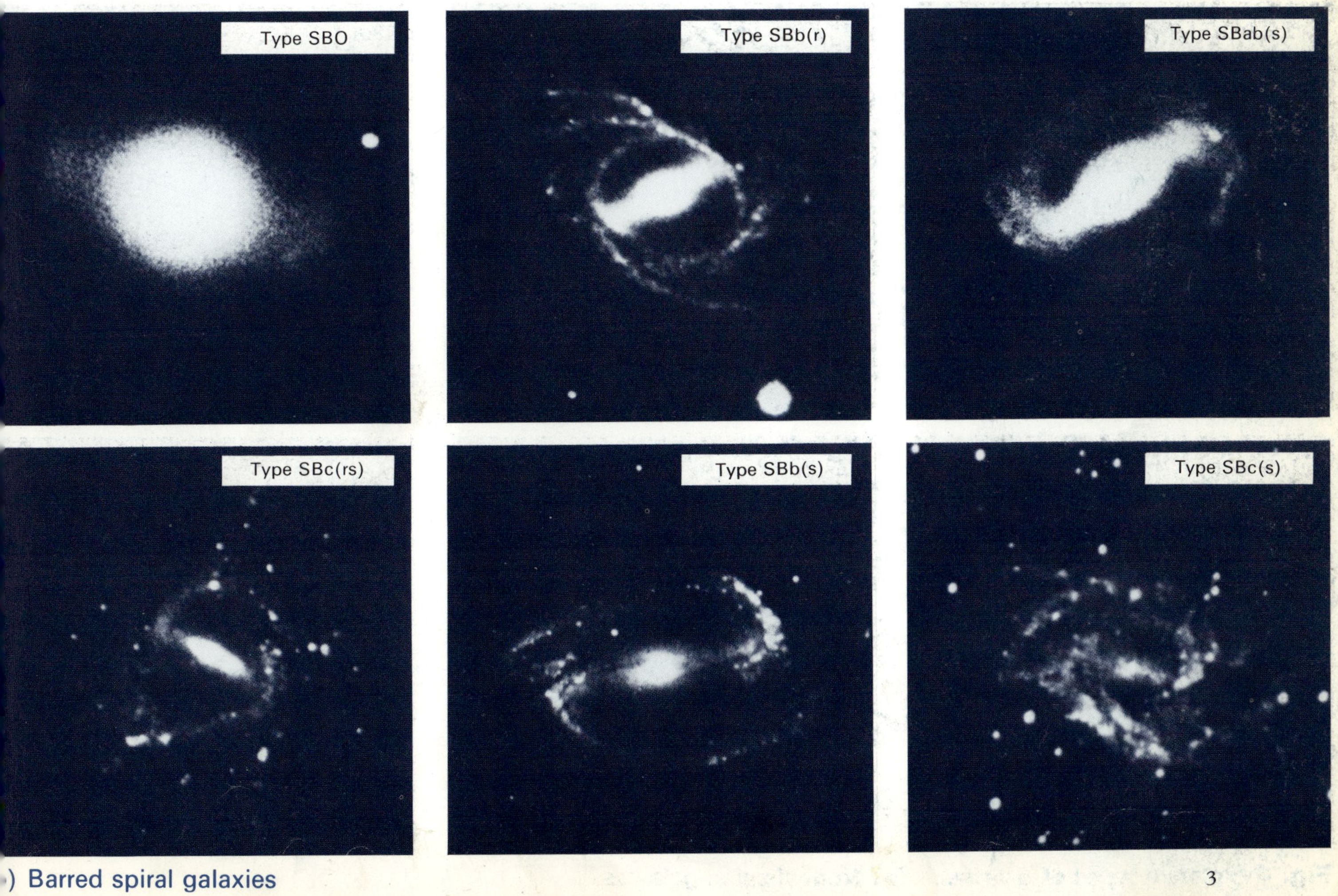

Type SBO
Type SBb(r)
Type SBab(s)
Type SBc(rs)
Type SBb(s)
Type SBc(s)

) Barred spiral galaxies

besides our Milky Way. Galaxies come in different shapes and sizes, and they are always grouped in clusters. Distances between galaxies in a cluster are vast (about 10 times the size of any galaxy, i.e. about seven million billion* kilometres), but these distances are small compared with the distances between clusters.

   * a billion = a million million

So the universe can be seen as a collection of a large number of clusters of galaxies, each cluster containing between 20 and 100 galaxies, each galaxy consisting of a very large number of stars. In our Milky Way we are familiar with the star which has a solar system (our Sun). We also know quite a lot about our own Earth, and we are getting to know the other planets in the Solar System with the help of space probes.

Fig. 5 A galaxy similar to our own Milky Way

Before you start

The projects in this book are carefully arranged in order, but you do not have to follow this sequence – just do the projects as they interest you. However, you will find that some later projects depend on information or equipment found or made in earlier projects and you may need to refer back to these. Some of the information can be found in other ways. For example, you can find latitude from an atlas or a map of the area where you live. You can get an idea of direction by using a magnetic compass. But I hope that the projects, as well as being fun, will give you a good understanding of some basic astronomical ideas.

There are some technical terms, which are mostly explained as we go along, but there is a short glossary at the back of the book if you need it (Appendix 1).

Most of the materials can be bought cheaply from hardware, stationery or do-it-yourself shops, but for the telescopes and binoculars you will need more specialised shops. A short list of suppliers is given in Appendix 2.

You can get a lot of fun from astronomy as a hobby, but even more if you join a local group of amateur astronomers – you can learn a great deal this way too. Appendix 3 gives details of astronomical societies who would be able to give you the address of your local group. You may also find, while working through this book, that you want to learn more about a particular part of astronomy: in Appendix 4 you will find a short list of books which could help you to do this.

There are not many books devoted to learning astronomy through making equipment and observing for yourself, so I hope you will find this one a refreshing change and will enjoy the activities presented in it. An exciting fact to remember about astronomy is that although professional astronomers use complicated instruments on a large variety of special telescopes, the amateur astronomer can still make important contributions with simple instruments. For example, *novae* and *supernovae* are special stars that suddenly increase their brightness over a period of days and several of these were first observed by amateurs. Amateur astronomers have also discovered new comets, so even with the simple methods described in this book, you can not only learn a lot of astronomy, but also perhaps start on the road towards an important astronomical discovery.

Many happy hours of making, doing and observing, and good luck for your own real discovery!

PROJECT 1 Shadows cast by the Sun

For hundreds of years people have used the shadows cast by the Sun to tell the time. Some used shadow clocks or sundials, others could tell the time by the lengths of their own shadows. In this project we see how the length and direction of the shadow of an upright stick will change as the day goes by.

What you need

A level surface in a sunny outside spot, preferably tiled or cemented, on which a 2 metre square can be marked (failing that, a piece of plywood 2 m square, 5 mm thick); thin straight piece of bamboo or other stick about 50 cm long; small flowerpot filled with soil; plumbline; spirit level; steel tape-measure; graph paper; watch; protractor; chalk or pencil; string.

What to do

Day 1: the aim is to measure the changing length of the shadow cast by the Sun of the bamboo stick.

1   Measure and make a note of the *radius* of the flowerpot base.

2   Use spirit level to check that the surface is level. If not, use piece of plywood and build up underneath on one side or other until quite level.

3   Put stick into centre of flowerpot and make sure it is absolutely vertical using the plumbline as a guide (see fig. 1.1).

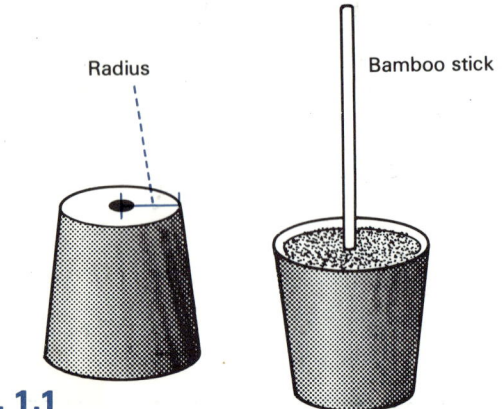

Fig. 1.1

4   From your general knowledge of where the Sun rises and sets, or from a map of your area, you will have a rough idea of the East–West and North–South directions. Mark out a 2 m square on the level area or line up plywood so that the edges are running approximately North–South and East–West (making sure to keep it level). Place flowerpot midway along southernmost edge of area or plywood (see fig. 1.2).

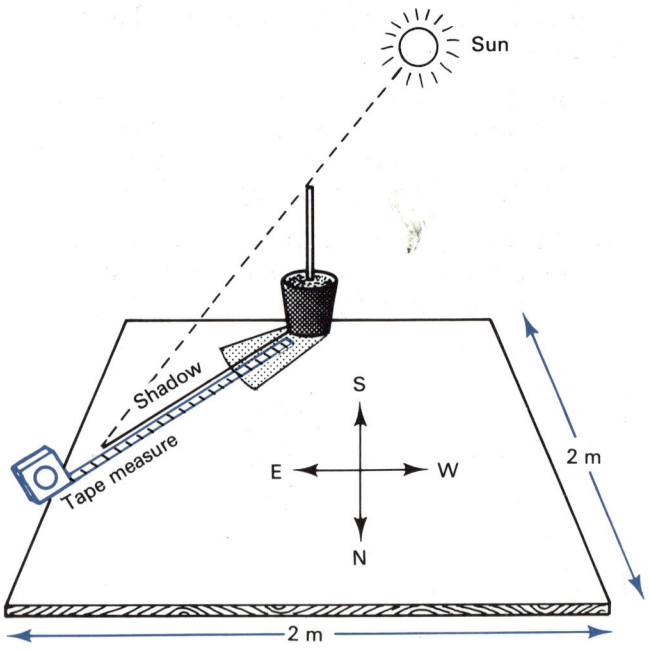

Fig. 1.2

5   Starting at about 9.00 a.m. measure length of shadow of stick at hourly intervals. Use *Greenwich Mean Time* (GMT) and remember to subtract one hour if you are on British Summer Time. Measure along the shadow from the base of the flowerpot as shown in fig. 1.2. Each time you measure, add the radius of the flowerpot base to your measurement.

6   Plot your results on the graph paper using 1 mm to represent 1 cm of shadow length (see fig. 1.3). You will notice from your graph that the shadow length first decreases

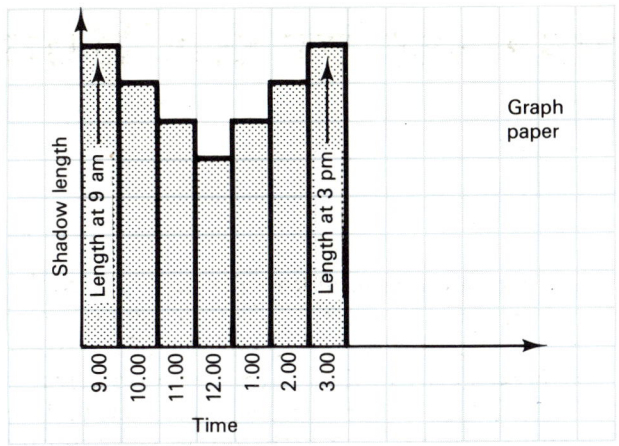

Shadow length · Length at 9 am · Length at 3 pm · Time · Graph paper

9.00 10.00 11.00 12.00 1.00 2.00 3.00

Fig. 1.3

until about 12 noon (GMT) and then increases again in the afternoon.

Day 2: We can now find the North–South line precisely.

7   Keeping flowerpot in position, draw a circle round base on the ground. Remove flower-pot and mark a dot in the centre of this circle. Call the dot C. Replace flowerpot.

8   At about 11 a.m. measure and draw the line of shadow cast by the stick. Call the tip of this line A (see fig. 1.4a).

9   Remove flowerpot. Tie chalk or pencil to one end of a piece of string. Hold string on centre mark of flowerpot circle. Keeping string taut and exactly the same length as from point A to point C, mark out a semi-circle on the ground, as shown in fig. 1.4b. Replace flowerpot.

10   You will notice the shadow getting shorter towards noon and then lengthening again. Watch the shadow until it once again touches the semi-circle you have drawn. Draw in this shadow line and call the point where the tip touches the circle point B.

11   Remove flowerpot, and extend the two lines until they meet at C.

12   Bisect the angle ACB. This line is pointing due North and South.

If you watch the shadow on another day, you will observe that the shadow is at its shortest just about when it crosses this North–South line. Note that the shortest shadow does not neces-sarily occur exactly at noon. Do you know why?

It would be a good idea, if possible, to mark the North–South line in some permanent way, because you will need to know this in some of the other projects.

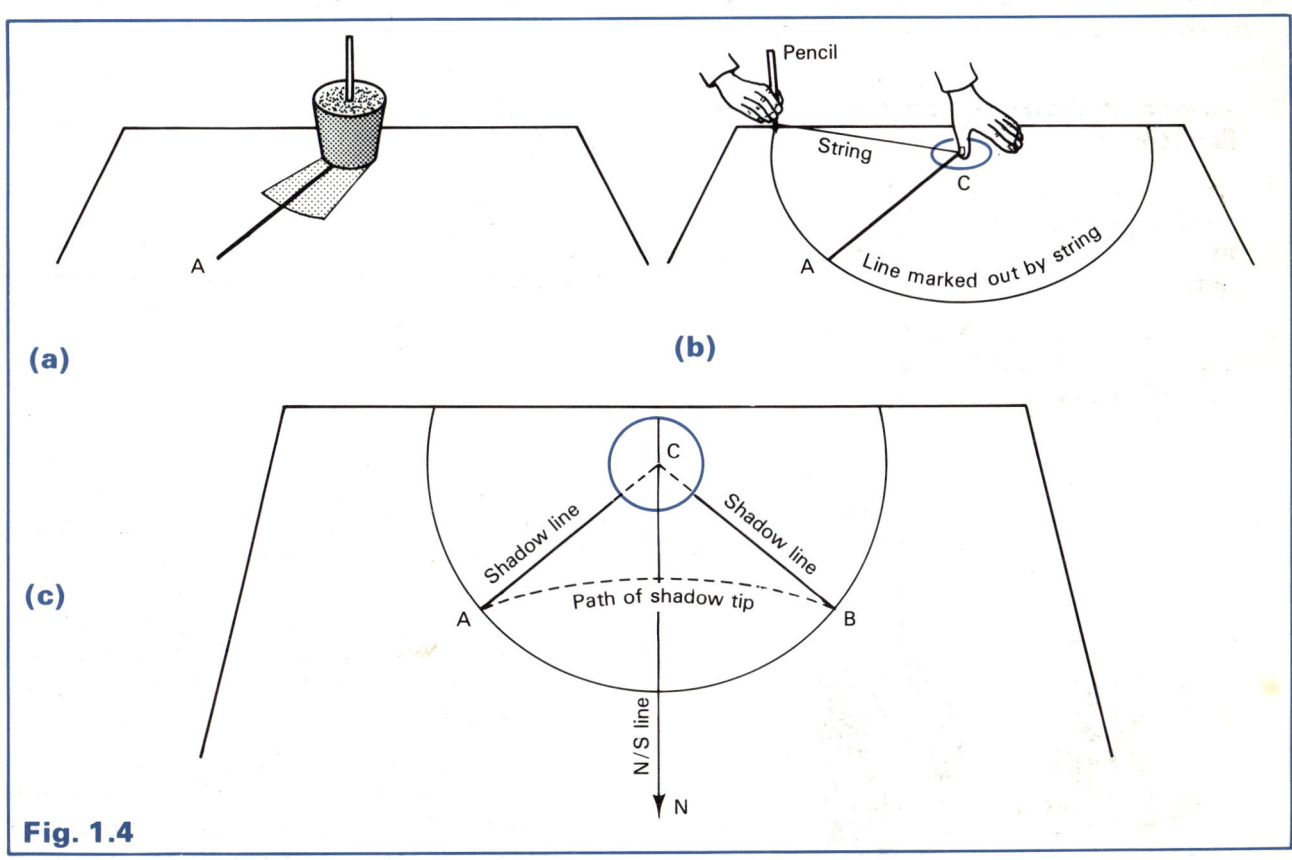

Pencil · String · C · A · Line marked out by string

(a)   (b)

(c)   C · Shadow line · Shadow line · A · Path of shadow tip · B · N/S line · N

Fig. 1.4

PROJECT 2   The length of the shortest shadow on different days of the year

The length of the shortest shadow will vary as the year goes by. This has been known for centuries and it is quite likely that people very long ago used varying shadow length as a kind of calendar. In this project we will find out how the length of the shadow changes with the dates of the year. This project will take one year to complete.

What you need

Materials used in the last project.

What to do

1 Set up the experiment as you did in the last project, with the North–South line clearly marked.

2 This time, measure the length of the shadow as it crosses the North–South line, using the same method as before. Make this measurement at least once a month, as close as possible to the 21st of each month.

3 Use the table below to record your results.

Date	21 Jan	21 Feb	21 Mar	21 Apr	21 May	21 Jun	21 Jul	21 Aug	21 Sep	21 Oct	21 Nov	21 Dec
Shadow length												

4 On the graph paper plot the shadow length against the date (see fig. 2.1), using 1 mm to represent 1 cm actual shadow length. When is the shadow at its shortest, and when at its longest?

Fig. 2.1

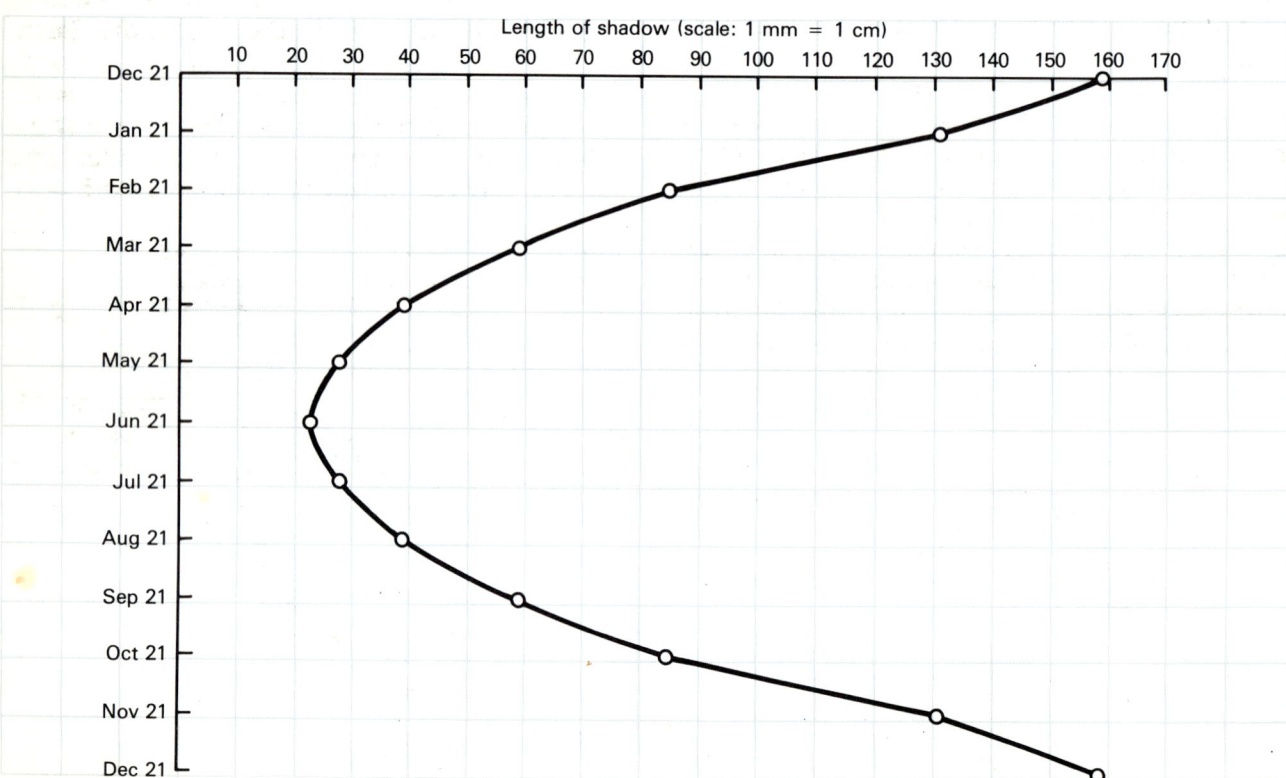

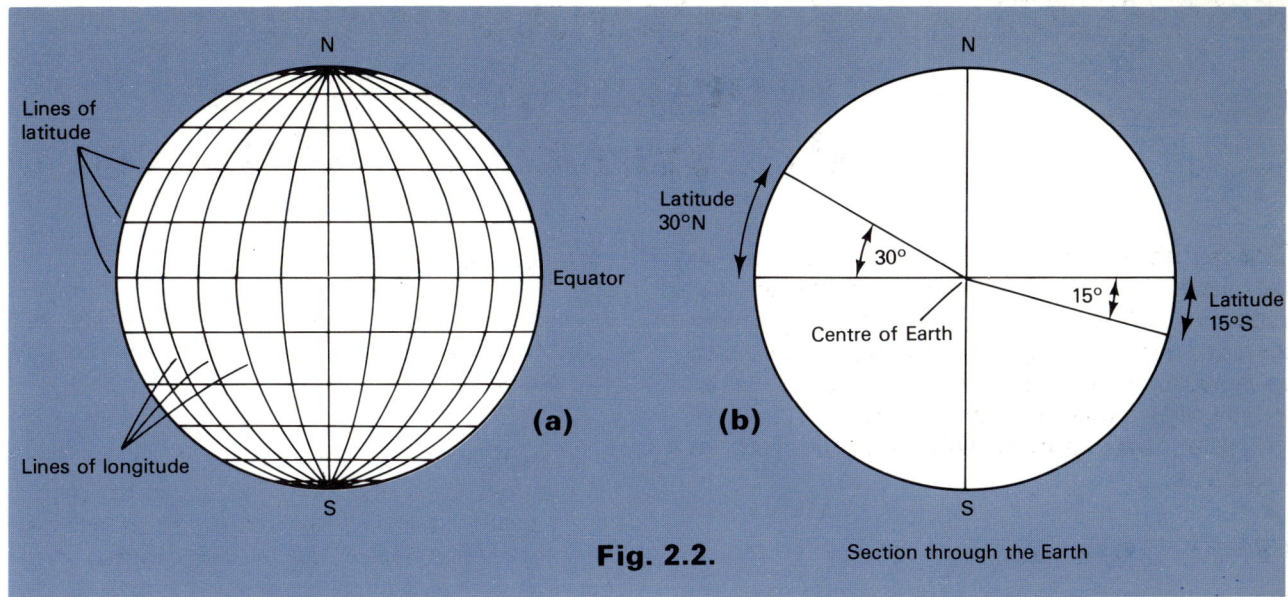

Fig. 2.2.   Section through the Earth

Finding latitude

If you look at a terrestrial globe you will notice lines going from the North Pole to the South Pole. These are called lines of *longitude*. There are also circles drawn right around the globe parallel to the *Equator*, which are lines of *latitude*. Latitude measures the distance north or south of the Equator in degrees (see figs. 2.2*a* and *b*). The latitude of the Equator is 0° while that of the North Pole is 90° north and that of the South Pole is 90° south. Longitude is also measured in degrees but this time it is degrees east or west of the line passing through Greenwich (called the *Greenwich Meridian*).

You can find your own latitude quite easily. Check the length of the shadow of your shadow stick on either 21 March or 23 September. Also measure very accurately the height of the top of the shadow stick above the level surface. Using the scale 1 mm to represent 1 cm of actual shadow length or actual stick length, draw the triangle as shown in fig. 2.3. Measure the angle at the top. The number of degrees in the angle is the same as the number of degrees that you are standing north or south of the Equator, and that is your latitude. Most of Western Europe lies between 40° and 70° north of the Equator: if you live in Plymouth, England, for example, your latitude is 50° north.

On 21 March and 23 September the Sun is directly overhead at some point on the Equator. Fig. 2.4 looks at the Earth from a point directly above the Equator but making an angle of 90° with the Sun. The Sun's distance from the Earth is very large compared with the size of the Earth so we can take the rays of light from the Sun to be parallel no matter where they strike the Earth. This means that the angle the Sun makes with the highest point in the sky (i.e. the point vertically overhead) is equal to the latitude of the place where the measurement is made. The highest point in the sky is called the *zenith*.

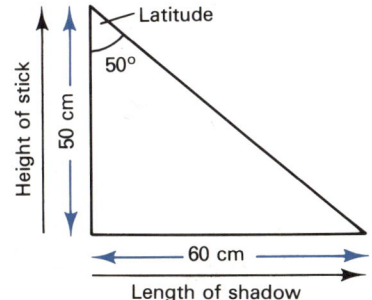

Fig. 2.3

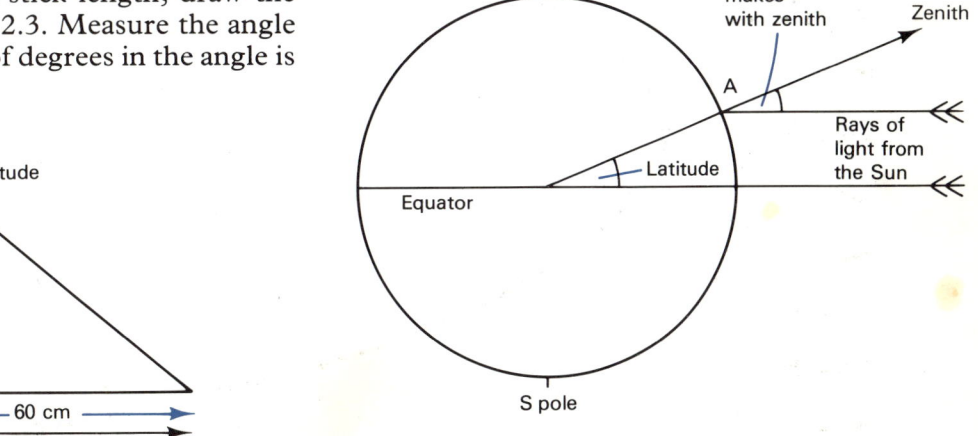

Fig. 2.4

PROJECT 3   Understanding latitude

This project describes a simple experiment to help understand the method of finding latitude used and described in the last project. A projector is used to represent the Sun and a large room or corridor is required to allow about 4 m between globe and projector, so that the rays from the projector can be regarded as parallel. In this project we use the Greenwich Meridian marked on the globe, but you can use any other line of longitude.

What you need

Globe of the Earth approx. 30 cm diameter; small slide projector; perspex disc 10 cm diameter (a circular protractor will do); graph paper; Blu-Tack.

What to do

1 Draw the figure shown in fig. 3.1 onto centimetre graph paper to dimensions given. Cut out around shape and also along line DC, and fold along dotted lines in the order 1, 2 and then 3.

2 Tuck in and glue DCFE to ABC to make figure shown in fig. 3.2. Note that GFC and BGC are at right angles to ABC, which is a *quadrant* (quarter circle).

3 Glue quadrant ABC to perspex disc as shown in fig. 3.3, making certain that point C is exactly at centre of disc.

4 Place globe at one end of large room with projector directly opposite as shown in fig. 3.4. Darken room and switch on projector.

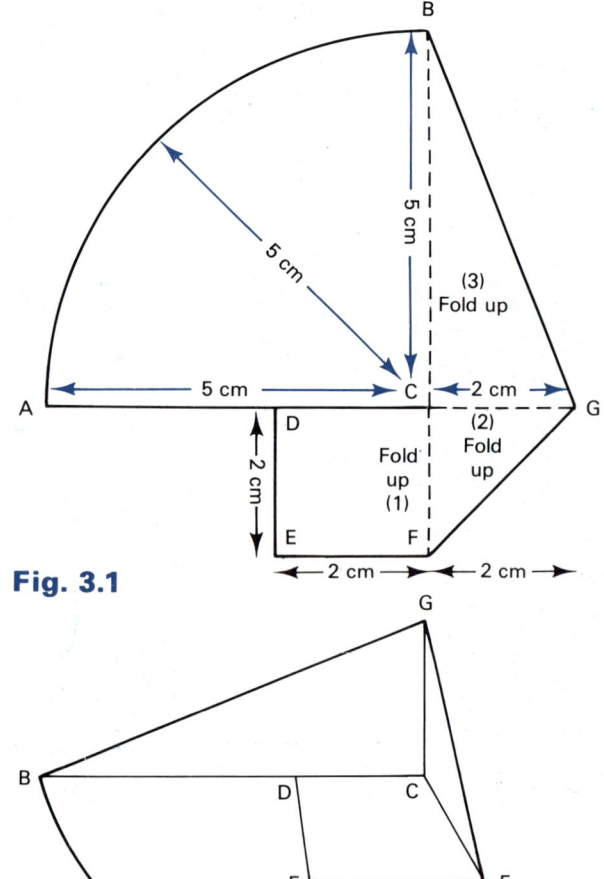

Fig. 3.1

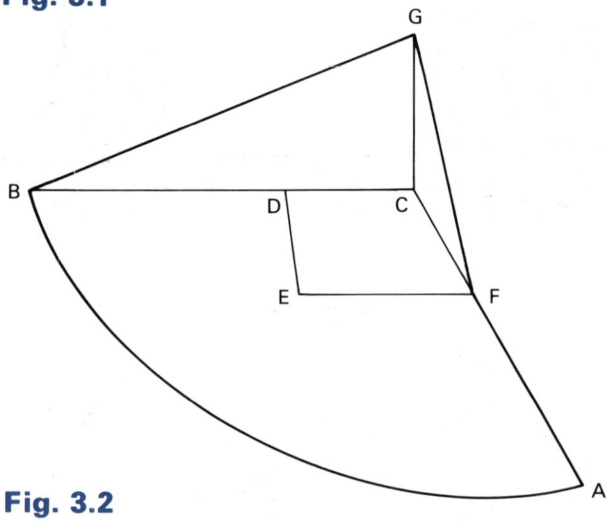

Fig. 3.2

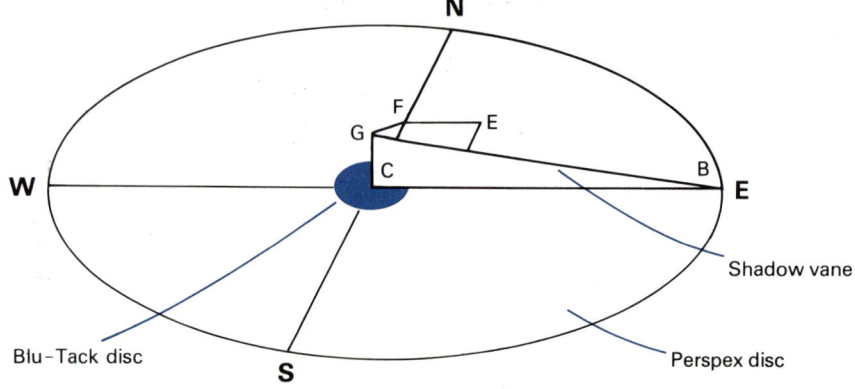

Fig. 3.3   Blu-Tack disc

10

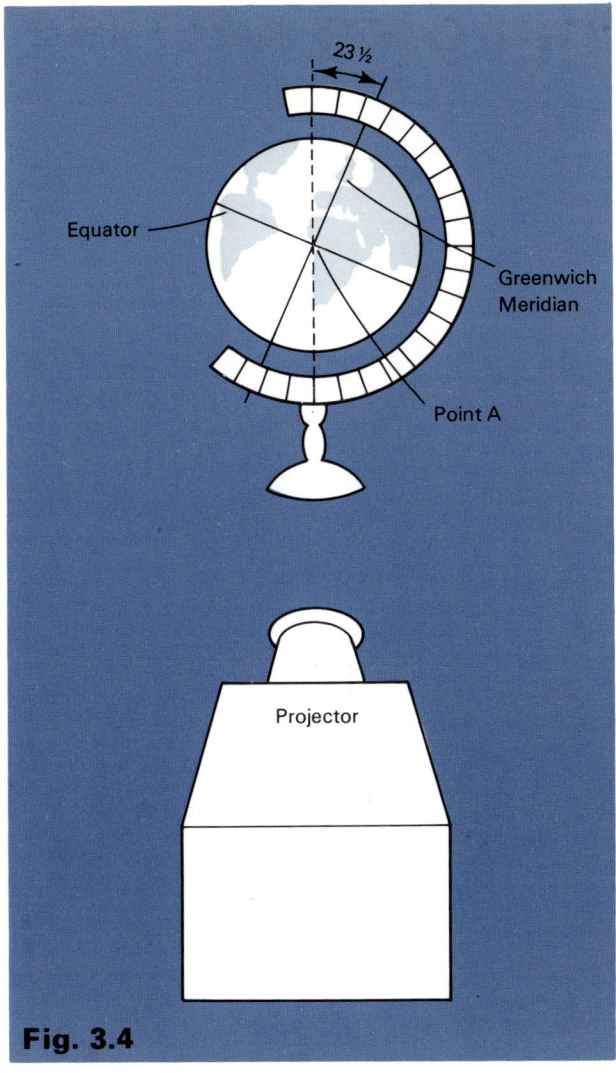

Fig. 3.4

5 Adjust globe so that line dividing light from dark passes through the poles and through 90° east and 90° west longitude (i.e. 90° either side of Greenwich Meridian). The point at which the Greenwich Meridian crosses the Equator should now be immediately opposite lens of projector. Call this point A.

6 With a small disc of Blu-Tack about 3 mm diameter, attach perspex disc to globe at point where 15° north latitude line crosses Greenwich Meridian. North, South, East and West on the disc should correspond to these directions on the globe (see fig. 3.5). If you have done this accurately the small triangle CGF should cast no shadow.

7 Measure and note length of shadow cast by edge of GC of larger triangle GCB (see fig. 3.5).

8 Move disc to point where latitude 23½° north crosses Greenwich Meridian. (This is the latitude of the Tropic of Cancer). Once again measure the length of the shadow cast by edge GC.

9 Repeat with the disc at latitudes 30° north, 45° north and 60° north.

10 Using the shadow length of GC, together with the actual length of the edge GC, draw a series of triangles, one for each latitude, and measure the angle at the top of each triangle as shown in fig. 3.6. In each case the angle should very nearly equal the latitude at which the measurement was made.

With a 30 cm diameter globe and a distance between globe and projector of 4 metres, the latitude worked out from the shadow length is within 2° of the globe latitude.

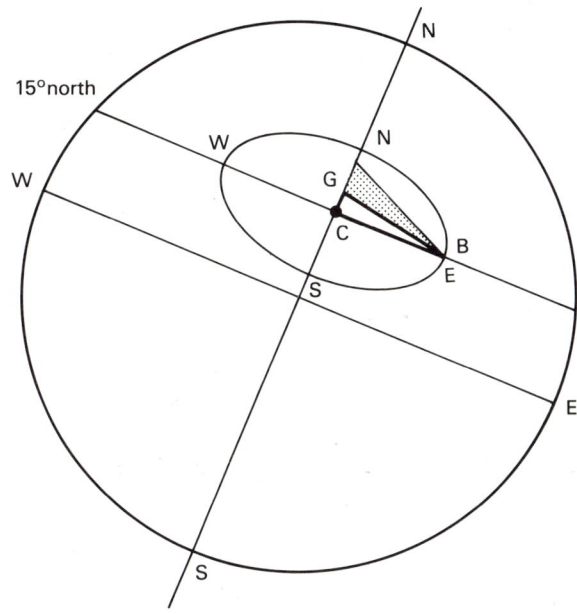

Fig. 3.5

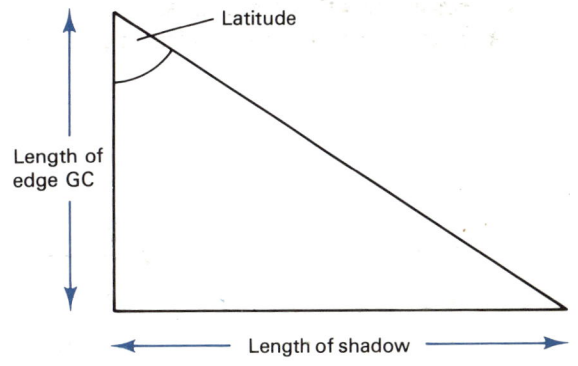

Fig. 3.6

PROJECT 4 Making and using sundials

We have already seen that the length and direction of shadows cast by the Sun change with time of day, so these shadows can be used to tell the time. This is the purpose of the sundial. In this project you will learn how to make and use two different types of sundial.

What you need

Two pieces of wood: one 15 cm × 15 cm × 1.3 cm; one 7.6 cm × 7.6 cm × 7.6 cm; cardboard; protractor; plastic drinking straw; small hand-saw; glue.

What to do

Sundial 1: Draw the face of the dial to the size shown in fig. 4.2 onto a piece of card, making sure the hours are spaced as shown. Glue this firmly to the wood 15 cm square. With small saw cut a groove through card and into wood along the north–south line, overlapping centre by about 3 mm. Now cut out a card triangle about the size and shape given in fig. 4.3, but making sure that angle A is equal to your own latitude (you found this in Project 2).

Glue the card triangle into position in the grove as shown in fig. 4.4, making sure that the inner corner A is exactly at the centre of your dial. This triangle, which casts a shadow onto the face of the sundial, is called a *gnomon*. To use the sundial, first place it on a level surface and then turn it so that the north–south line is correctly aligned with your permanent north–south direction line (Project 1). The place where the shadow of the edge of the gnomon falls on the face of the dial will give you the time (GMT).

Sundial 2: Draw the second sundial onto a piece of card and cut out along the heavy black lines and between the tags marked X (see fig. 4.5). Punch out the holes marked in the centres of the circles, big enough to hold a drinking straw. Fold the tags upwards along dotted lines and then the two circles. Bend the ends of the rectangle W, E, E′, W′ upward to form half a cylinder and glue the back of the tags to the edges of the half-cylinder, as shown in fig. 4.6.

Saw wooden block to shape as shown in fig. 4.7, so that angle B is equal to your latitude. Mark out a circle of same diameter as semi-cylinder on the slope you have made, and drill a hole in the centre of the circle big enough to hold drinking straw. Mark east and west points on a horizontal line passing through centre hole.

Glue base of semi-cylinder to block so that E and W points coincide and so that hole in base coincides with hole in block. Put a little glue on the end of the straw and pass straw through both holes in semi-cylinder and into hole in block of wood (see fig. 4.8).

To use the sundial, place the flat base of the block on a level surface with the E–W line at right angles to your N–S direction line and with inside of semi-cylinder facing south. The shadow of the straw on the inner curved surface of the semi-cylinder will give you the time (GMT).

The apparent pathway of the Sun through the sky is curved and the Sun moves through 15° each hour. If we have a gnomon (in this case the straw) at right angles to the Sun's path and the shadow of the gnomon falls on a curved surface, the shadow will also move through 15° each hour. This explains why the time lines on the semi-cylindrical sundial are evenly spaced (see fig. 4.1). If, however, the dial face is flat and horizontal, then the time lines are not equally spaced (see fig. 4.2).

Fig. 4.1

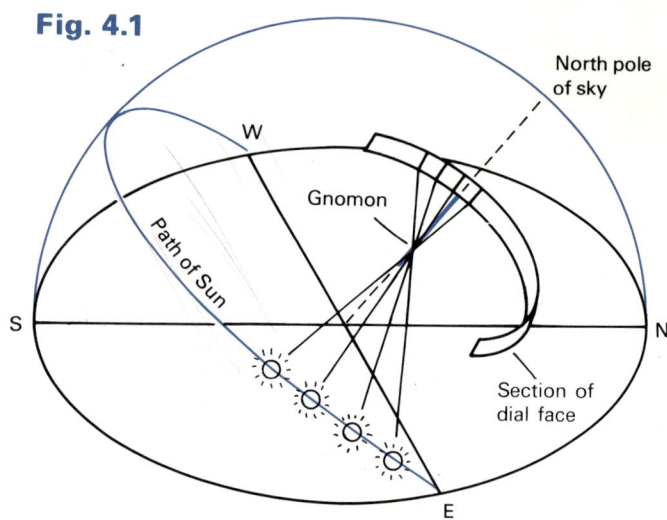

SUNDIAL 1—PLANS AND CONSTRUCTION

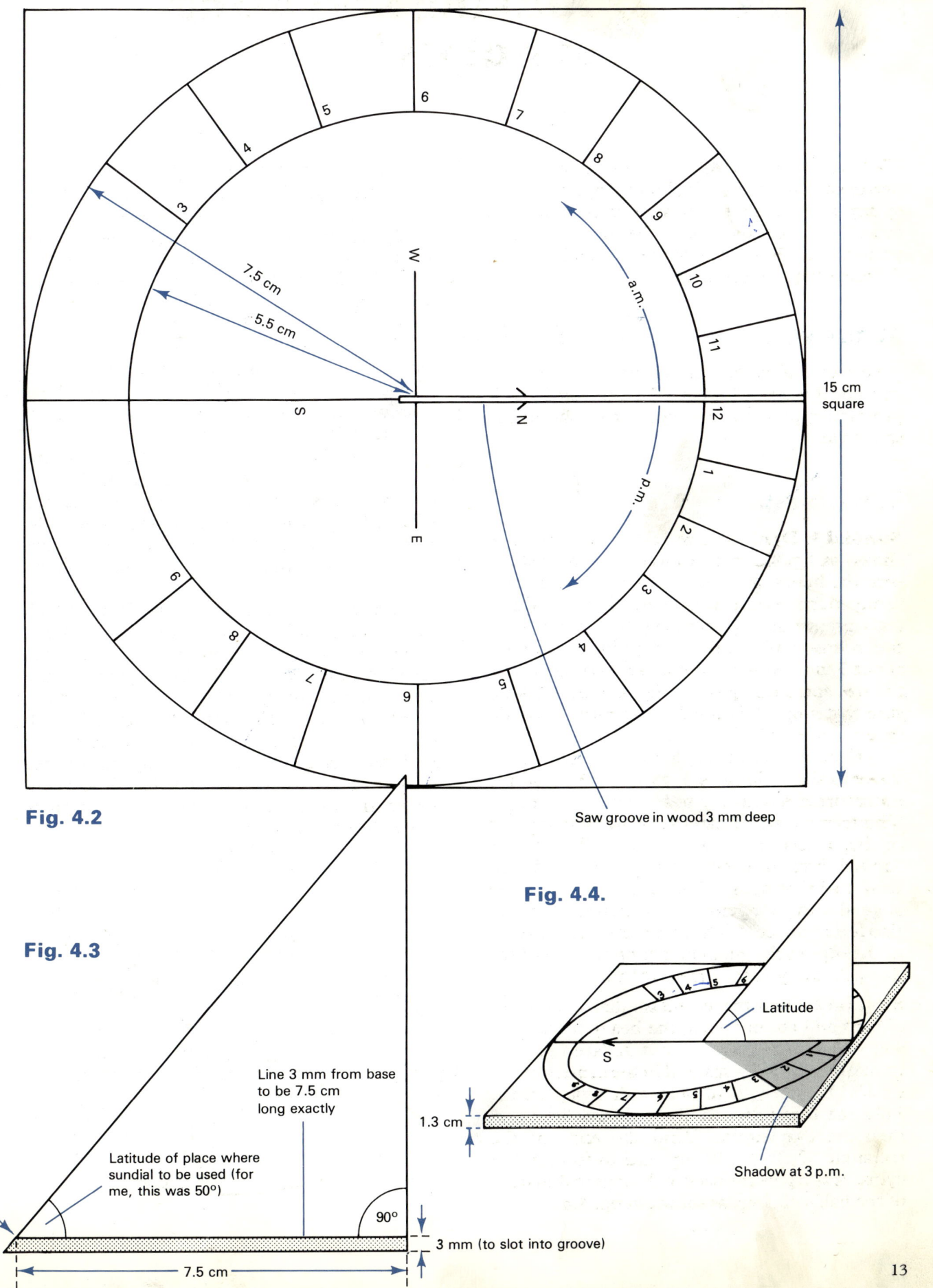

Fig. 4.2

7.5 cm

5.5 cm

W

S

N

E

a.m.

p.m.

15 cm square

6 5 4 3 7 8 9 10 11 12 1 2 3 4 5 6 7 8 9

Saw groove in wood 3 mm deep

Fig. 4.3

Line 3 mm from base to be 7.5 cm long exactly

Latitude of place where sundial to be used (for me, this was 50°)

A

90°

3 mm (to slot into groove)

7.5 cm

Fig. 4.4.

Latitude

S

1.3 cm

Shadow at 3 p.m.

SUNDIAL 2—PLANS AND CONSTRUCTION

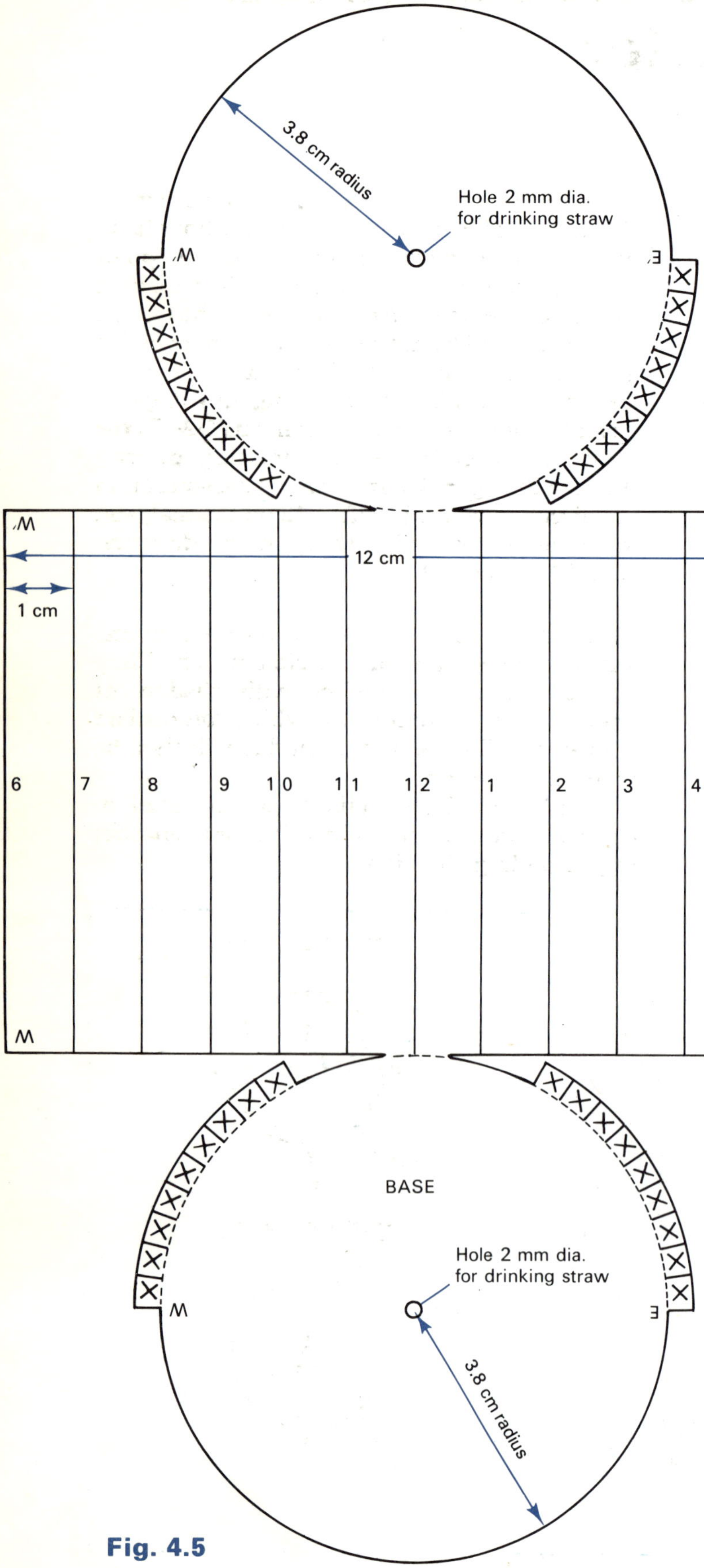

3.8 cm radius

Hole 2 mm dia. for drinking straw

W'

E'

W

12 cm

1 cm

E

8 cm

| 6 | 7 | 8 | 9 | 10 | 11 | 12 | 1 | 2 | 3 | 4 | 5 | 6 |

W

E

BASE

Hole 2 mm dia. for drinking straw

3.8 cm radius

W

E

Fig. 4.5

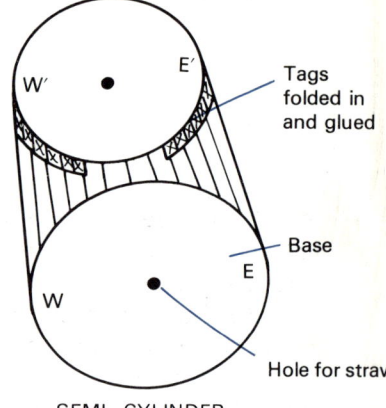

Tags folded in and glued

W'

E'

Base

W

E

Hole for straw

SEMI—CYLINDER

Fig. 4.6

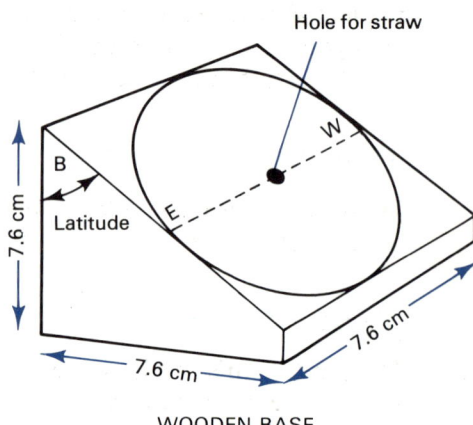

Hole for straw

7.6 cm

B

Latitude

W

E

7.6 cm

7.6 cm

WOODEN BASE

Fig. 4.7

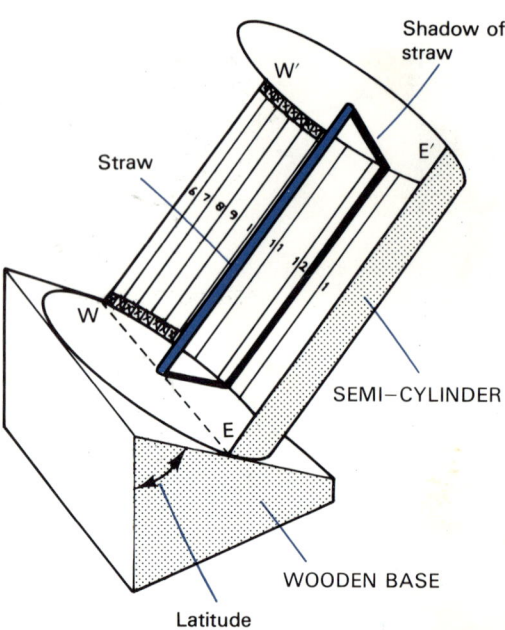

Shadow of straw

W'

E'

Straw

W

E

SEMI—CYLINDER

WOODEN BASE

Latitude

Fig. 4.8

PROJECT 5   Using the Sun to find direction

We have already seen that the Sun not only changes its height above the horizon as the day goes by, but also changes direction in the sky. (As the Earth is spinning on its own axis, the heavenly bodies appear to change their directions with respect to us.) In this project we see that the Sun can be used to find direction provided one has another method of telling the time. There are two ways of doing this. This project always refers to Greenwich Mean Time, so if you are on British Summer Time remember you are one hour ahead of GMT.

What you need

Wristwatch; Sundial No. 1 (see Project 4); spirit level; matchstick.

What to do

Method 1: this method uses a watch with a dial face. Place the watch on a level surface. Hold the matchstick at right angles to surface and very close to rim of watch face. Keeping the match-

stick steady, turn the watch until the shadow of the stick cast by the Sun lies along the hour hand of watch. The tip of the hour hand should point to the place where the matchstick just touches the rim of the watch. At the centre of the face an angle is formed by the shadow of the matchstick and the line joining 12 to the centre (or 1 if you are on BST). The line bisecting this angle is along the north–south line. At noon (GMT) the south direction is the one pointing directly through the figure 12. In the morning south is in the direction which is before 12 on the dial, and in the afternoon and evening in the direction after 12 (see fig. 5.1).

Method 2: this method is more accurate, and can be used with a digital watch. Place sundial on a level surface with shadow of gnomon pointing to the time which you read on your watch. The N on the sundial will then be pointing due north.

Either of these methods can be used to check a magnetic compass bearing, or as another way of finding direction.

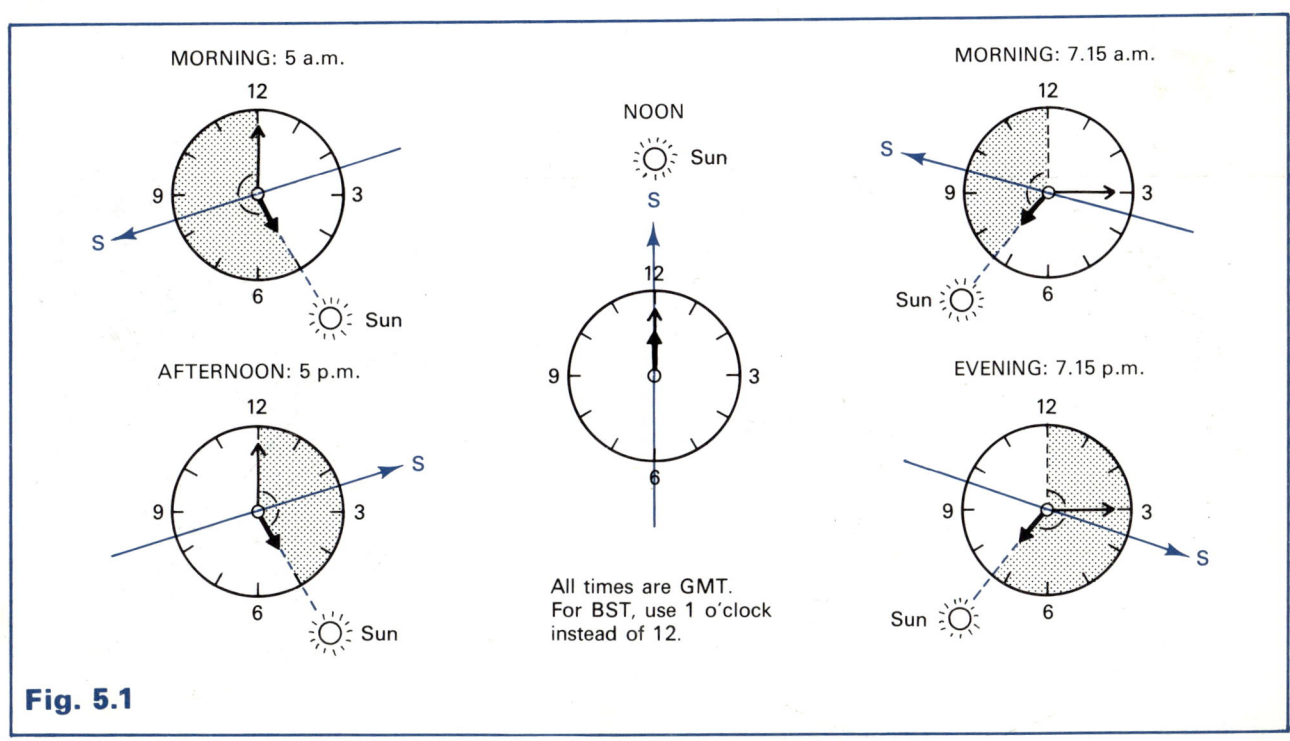

Fig. 5.1

PROJECT 6   Finding out how stars move across the sky

Like the Sun, stars also change their heights above the horizon and their directions as the night goes by, but they are, of course, too faint to cast shadows. However, with a very simple instrument we can see how they move across the sky. In this project we will make the instrument and then use it to find out how the stars move.

What you need

Circular protractor 10 cm diameter; semi-circular protractor 10 cm diameter; wooden batten 2 cm × 2 cm × 12.6 cm; another piece of wood 15 cm × 15 cm × 1.2 cm; drill; stiff card; four 6 mm screws; two drawing pins; strong cotton; small weight; graph paper; plain pin; sellotape.

What to do

1 Make a tube 10 cm long out of stiff card by rolling card round a pencil and sticking it with sellotape.

2 Drill a small hole just big enough to take shaft of drawing pin in the semi-circular protractor at the point where all the lines meet.

3 Attach cardboard to protractor along its straight edge (see fig. 6.1a).

4 Attach protractor to top of batten with drawing pin so that it moves easily but not too freely about shaft of pin (see fig. 6.1a).

5 Make a pointer on batten just below 0° point on protractor when tube is exactly horizontal.

6 Make a marker 4.5 cm long out of card and glue to base of batten.

7 Make a plumbline with cotton and small weight and fix this to opposite side of batten from protractor with plain pin (see fig. 6.1b).

8 Drill five holes into circular protractor at points shown in fig. 6.2a. Centre hole should be just big enough to take shaft of drawing pin; other holes should be big enough to take four 6 mm screws.

9 Fix base of batten to centre of circular

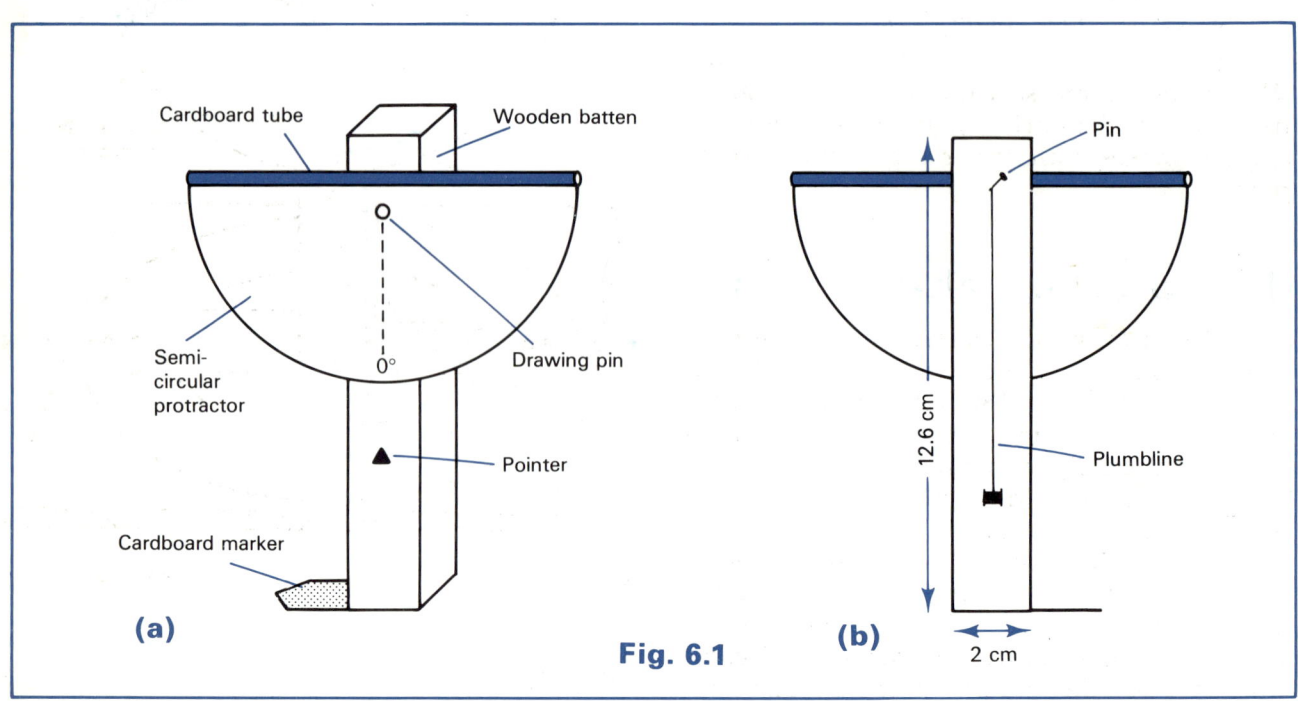

Fig. 6.1

(a)
- Cardboard tube
- Wooden batten
- Semi-circular protractor
- Drawing pin
- 0°
- Pointer
- Cardboard marker

(b)
- Pin
- 12.6 cm
- Plumbline
- 2 cm

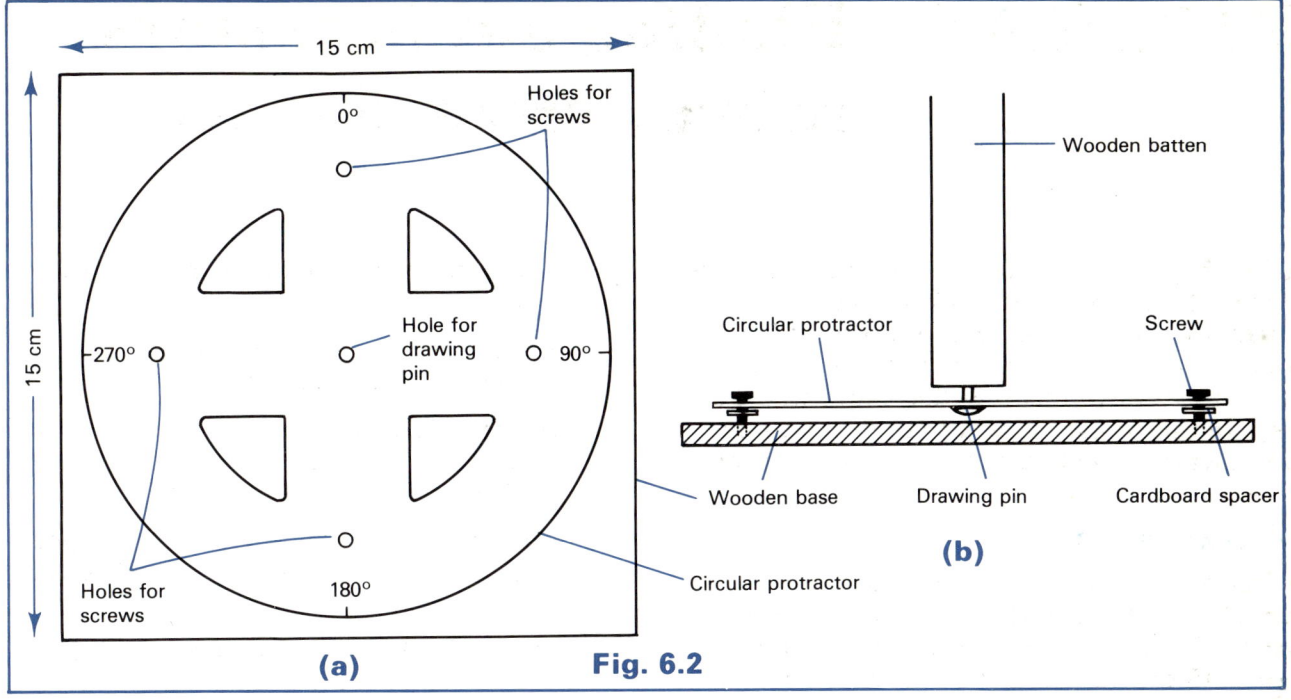

(a)   **Fig. 6.2**

protractor with drawing pin so that batten moves easily but not too freely.

10   Screw circular protractor to second piece of wood, using cardboard spacers to separate protractor from wooden base in order not to trap drawing pin (see fig. 6.2*b*).

11   Check that batten is vertical, i.e. that plumbline hangs exactly down centre of batten, as shown in fig. 6.1*b*.

This instrument is called an *alt-azimuth*. With it you can measure the *altitude* of a star (its height above the horizon), and its *azimuth* (the angle it makes with either the north or south points).

How to use the alt-azimuth

Place the alt-azimuth on a level surface with the 0° mark on the circular protractor pointing towards north and the 180° mark towards south. For your first experiment choose a star close to the east in the early evening, and follow this star for the rest of the evening, making observations every half hour, as follows.

Keeping the base firm, turn batten around and move protractor up or down until you can see your chosen star through the cardboard tube. The altitude is measured on the semi-circular protractor and the azimuth on the circular pro-

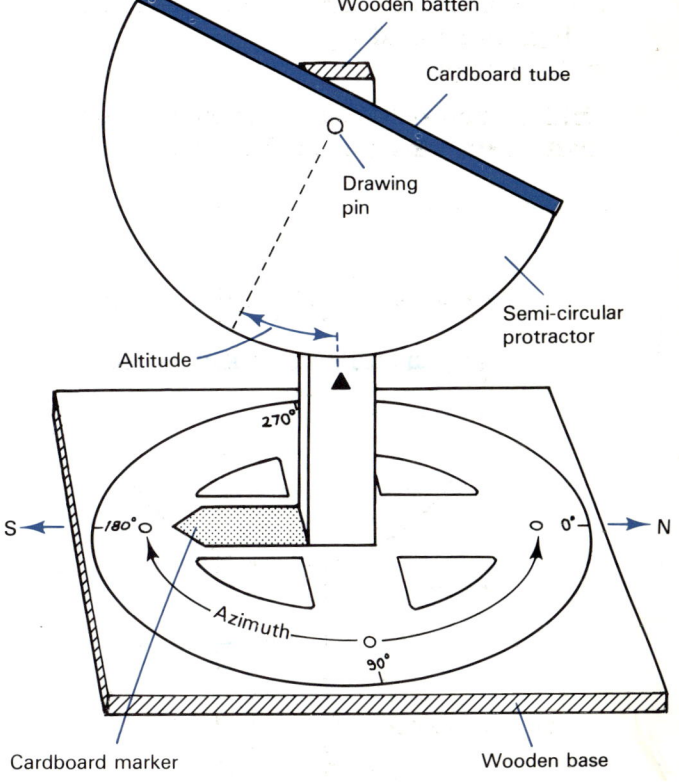

Fig. 6.3

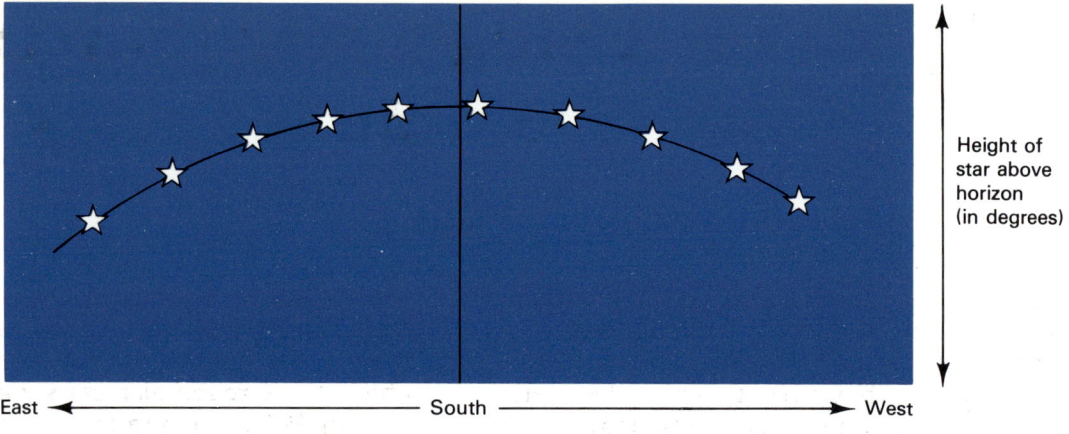

Fig. 6.4

East ◄——————— South ———————► West

Number of degrees star is east of south Number of degrees star is west of south

Height of star above horizon (in degrees)

tractor (see fig. 6.3). The azimuth angle is the angle between the marker and either the north or south points, depending on which way you are looking.

Plot your results on a sheet of graph paper. Divide the horizontal axis in half and on the left plot number of degrees east of south and on the right plot number of degrees west of south (see fig. 6.4). On the vertical axis plot the number of degrees that the star was above the horizon at a given time. If you join up the dots showing the different positions with a line, you should get a curve rising up as it crosses the south point on your graph and then sinking again towards the west. This graph shows you that the stars rise somewhere in the east, increasing their height above the horizon until they have reached the south, and after that they decrease their altitudes and finally set somewhere in the west.

Repeat the observations, this time taking a star which is low on the northern horizon at the start of the evening, and plot your results on another sheet of graph paper (see fig. 6.5). You should be able to see that this star makes part of a circle in the course of the evening. If you could watch this star for 24 hours it would complete a circle, and the centre of this circle is called the *pole* of the sky. (As we will see in Project 7, the *pole star* is extremely close to this central point.) All the stars in the sky appear to pivot around this central point if we watch them throughout the night. The stars very near to the pole of the sky, between the pole and the north point of your horizon, never in fact set: they just go around the pole in circles. If the star you chose was close to the pole of the sky it probably did not set at all. Stars which never set are called *circumpolar* stars, because they go round the pole of the sky.

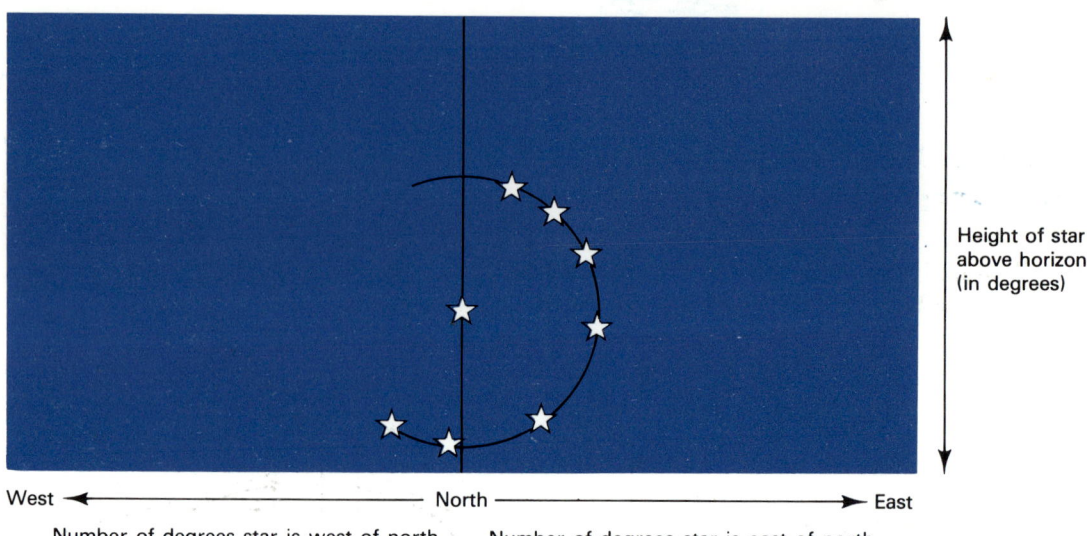

Fig. 6.5

West ◄——————— North ———————► East

Number of degrees star is west of north Number of degrees star is east of north

Height of star above horizon (in degrees)

PROJECT 7 Using a star map for the circumpolar stars

Long before people made maps of the Earth they had made maps of the sky (celestial maps). In fact the Greeks knew that before one could make a map of the Earth one had first to make a celestial map. In making these maps astronomers linked the brighter stars together to form imaginary shapes and patterns which they named after animals or birds they saw in the countryside, or after their heroes or gods.

Although the stars forming these shapes move across the sky as the Earth spins on its own axis, they do not seem to change their distances from each other as seen from the face of Earth over very long periods of time. These shapes are called *constellations*.

Stars vary in brightness, so astronomers call the brightest stars magnitude 0, and the faintest stars that can be seen without a telescope magnitude 6. In our star maps (at the front and back of the book and on pages 21, 24 and 25) we only give positions of stars between 0 and 5 magnitude, using the following code:

Magnitude 0 and 1

    ,,   2

    ,,   3

    ,,   4

    ,,   5

Finding the Pole Star and 'the Plough'

We will start by finding the Pole Star, and then use this to see how to find the Plough at different times of night during the four seasons of the year. The Pole Star is so called because it is very close to the pole of the sky, the point around which the circumpolar stars move. The Pole Star (or Polaris) is sometimes called the North Star because it is always above the north point, and we will use this fact to find it.

Place the alt-azimuth instrument which you made in Project 6 on a level surface with the 0° mark on the circular protractor pointing towards north and the marker pointing to 0° (see fig. 7.1). Tilt cardboard tube so that it is looking at a point above the horizon – the angle of tilt should be equal to your latitude. You should now be able to see the North Star through the tube. If not, try squinting along the outside of the tube, and provided that you have done the setting up fairly carefully, you should be able to see the North Star. If you can now imagine a clock face on the northern sky, with the North Star at its centre, it should be easy to find the Plough using fig. 7.2 to help you. These diagrams show you the positions of the Plough with respect to the North

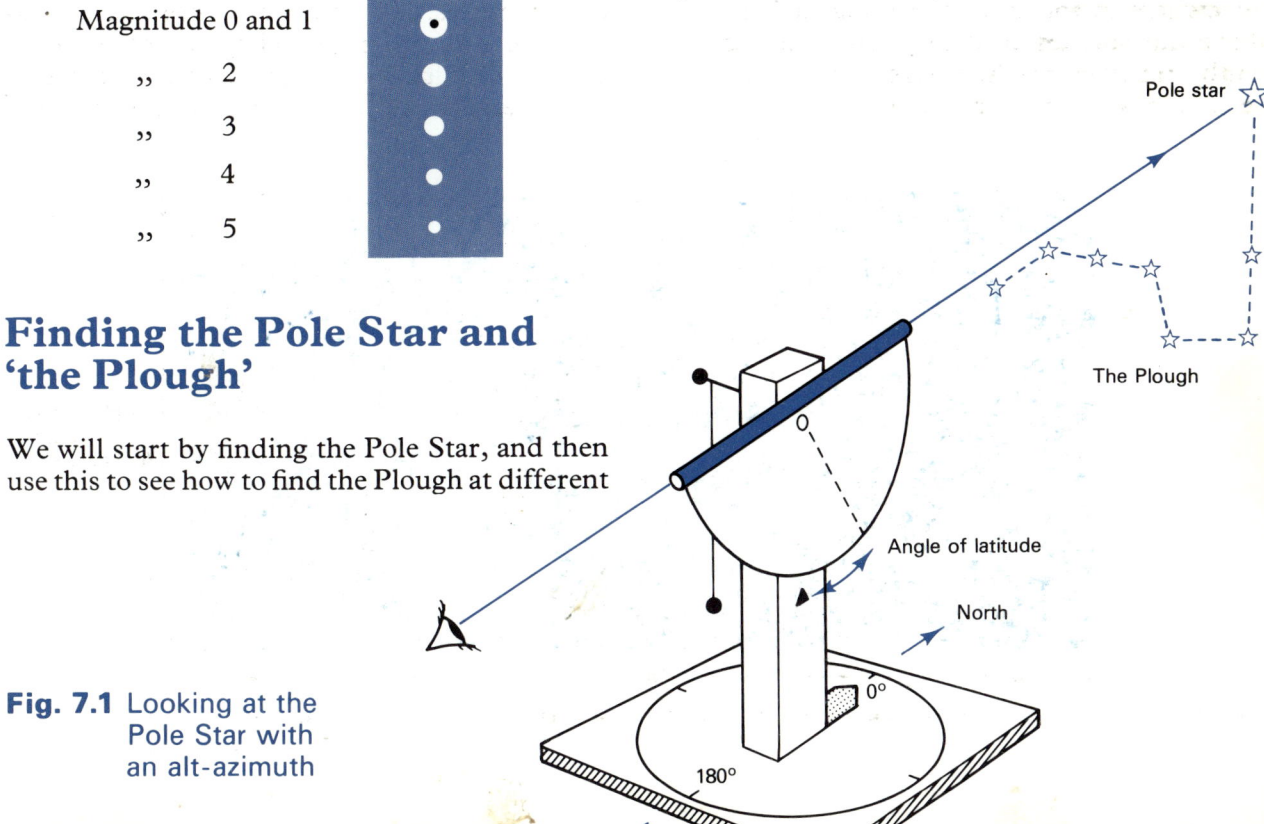

Fig. 7.1 Looking at the Pole Star with an alt-azimuth

Pole star

The Plough

Angle of latitude

North

0°

180°

South

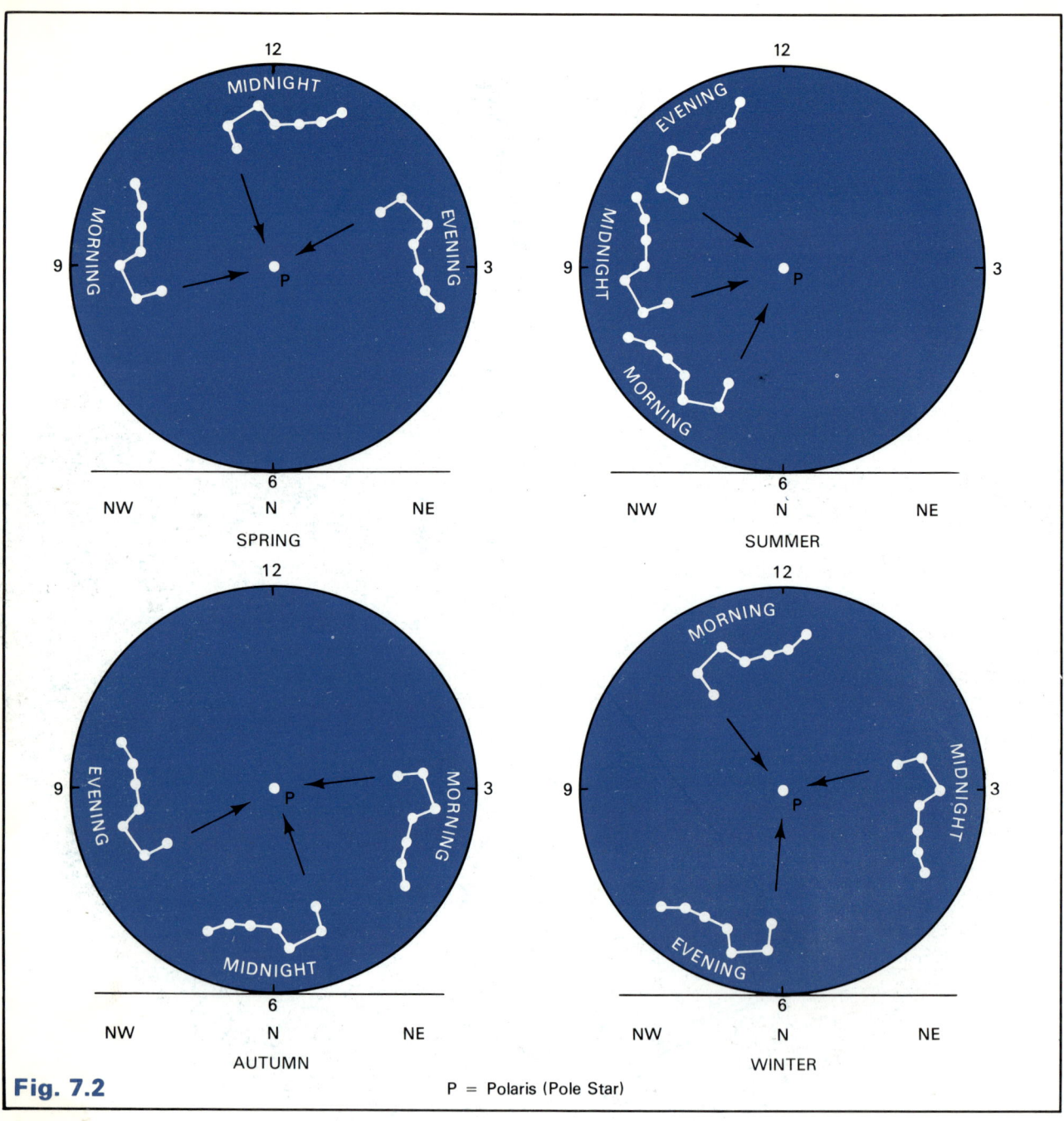

Fig. 7.2   P = Polaris (Pole Star)

Star at the beginning, middle and end of four nights of the year, one for each season.

Some people refer to the Plough as the Wagon, the Dipper or the Great Bear. Strictly speaking, the Great Bear is a larger constellation (called Ursa Major on the star map) which includes the stars of the Plough. Two of the stars of the Plough (see fig. 7.2) are called the pointers, because a straight line drawn through them and continued on would lead to the North Star.

Having found the Plough, you can now use the star map of the circumpolar stars (fig. 7.3) to find other well-known constellations. A particularly easy one to pick out is the W shape of Cassiopeia. It will be found on the opposite side of the Pole Star from the Plough. Another fairly easy constellation to find is Ursa Minor or the Little Bear. He is attached to the Pole Star by the tip of his tail. Most of the other constellations in this part of the sky are a bit harder to find, but the star map should help you, and with practice you will become familiar with the patterns in the night sky.

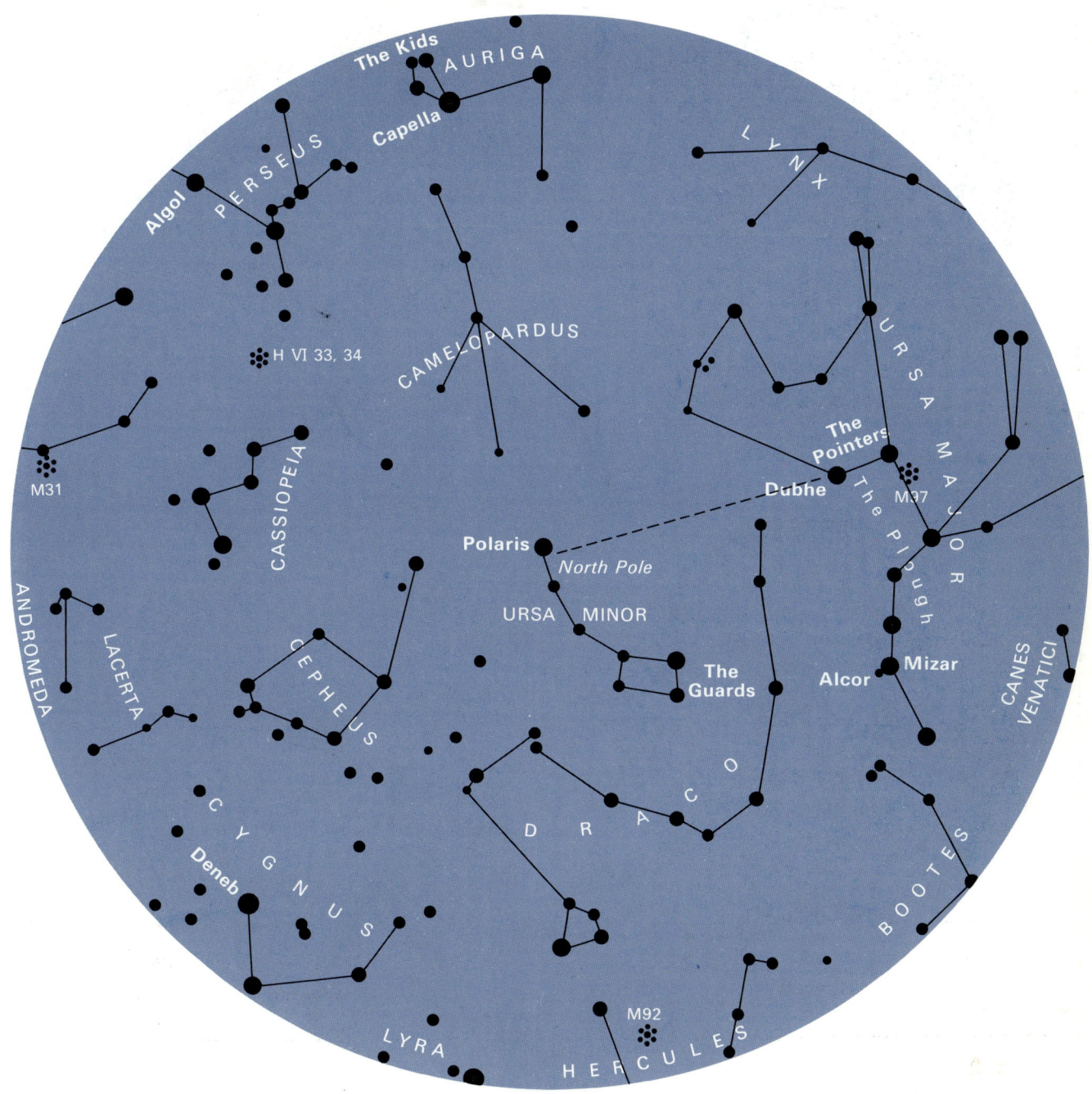

Fig. 7.3 Star map of the circumpolar region

PROJECT 8 Making and using a star clock

Just as we can use the Sun to tell the time during the day, so we can use the stars to tell the time at night. The Plough rotates round Polaris approximately once every 24 hours, but its starting point at a given time differs according to the seasons. These facts enable one to tell the time using a device called a *nocturnal*.

What you need

Stiff acetate film; brass paper fastener; masking tape.

What to do

Copy the three parts of the nocturnal, to dimensions given in fig. 8.3, onto acetate film and cut out. Punch a hole just big enough to take paper fastener through black dots on each part. Stick masking tape to the part of the arm shown shaded in the diagram. Assemble parts as shown in fig. 8.1.

Put in paper fastener. You now have a simple nocturnal.

Using the nocturnal

First make sure the pointer on the inner dial points to correct date on the outer dial. This is the date on which you are trying to find the time. Now, holding the nocturnal vertically, face north and cover Polaris – the North Star – with stud of paper fastener. Move the arm of the nocturnal until the two pointers of the Plough are just level with the lower edge of the arm (see fig. 8.2). Make sure that the dials are not moving about as you do this. The time can now be read against the lower edge of the arm on the inner dial.

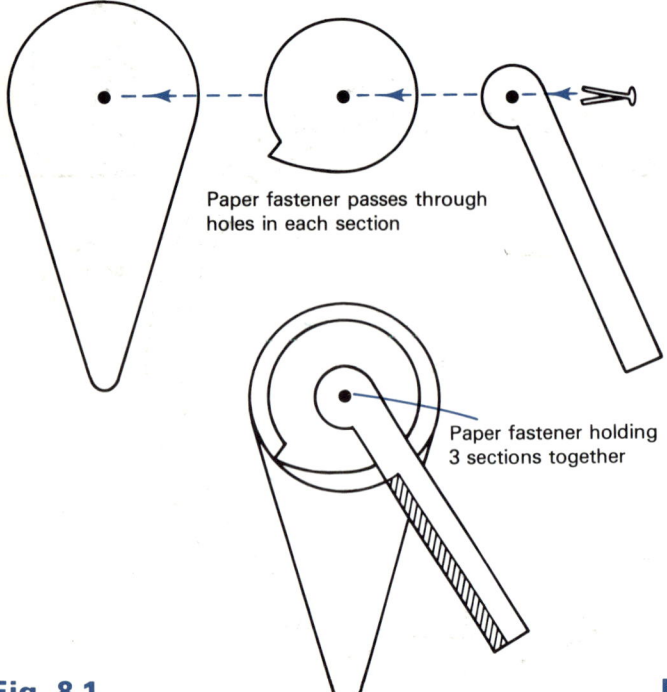

Paper fastener passes through holes in each section

Paper fastener holding 3 sections together

Fig. 8.1

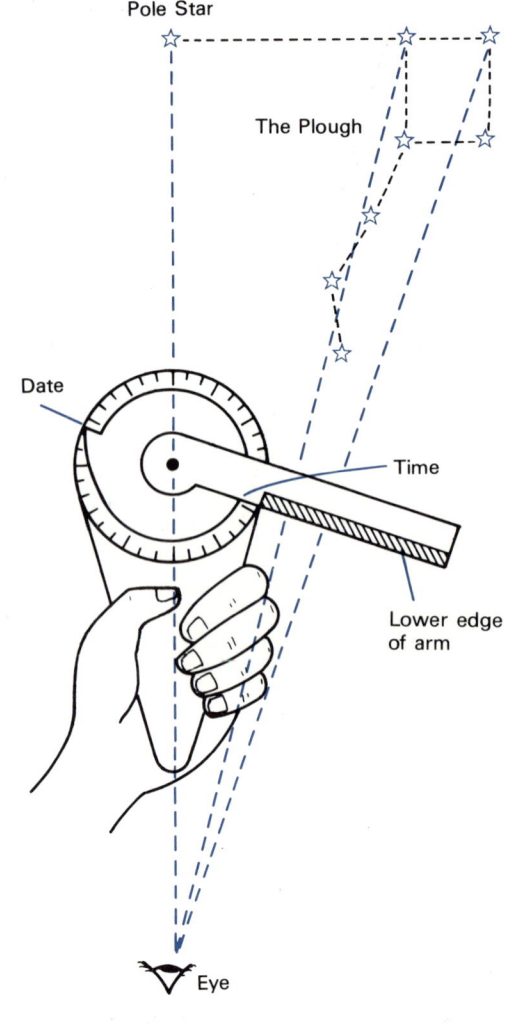

Pole Star

The Plough

Date

Time

Lower edge of arm

Eye

Fig. 8.2

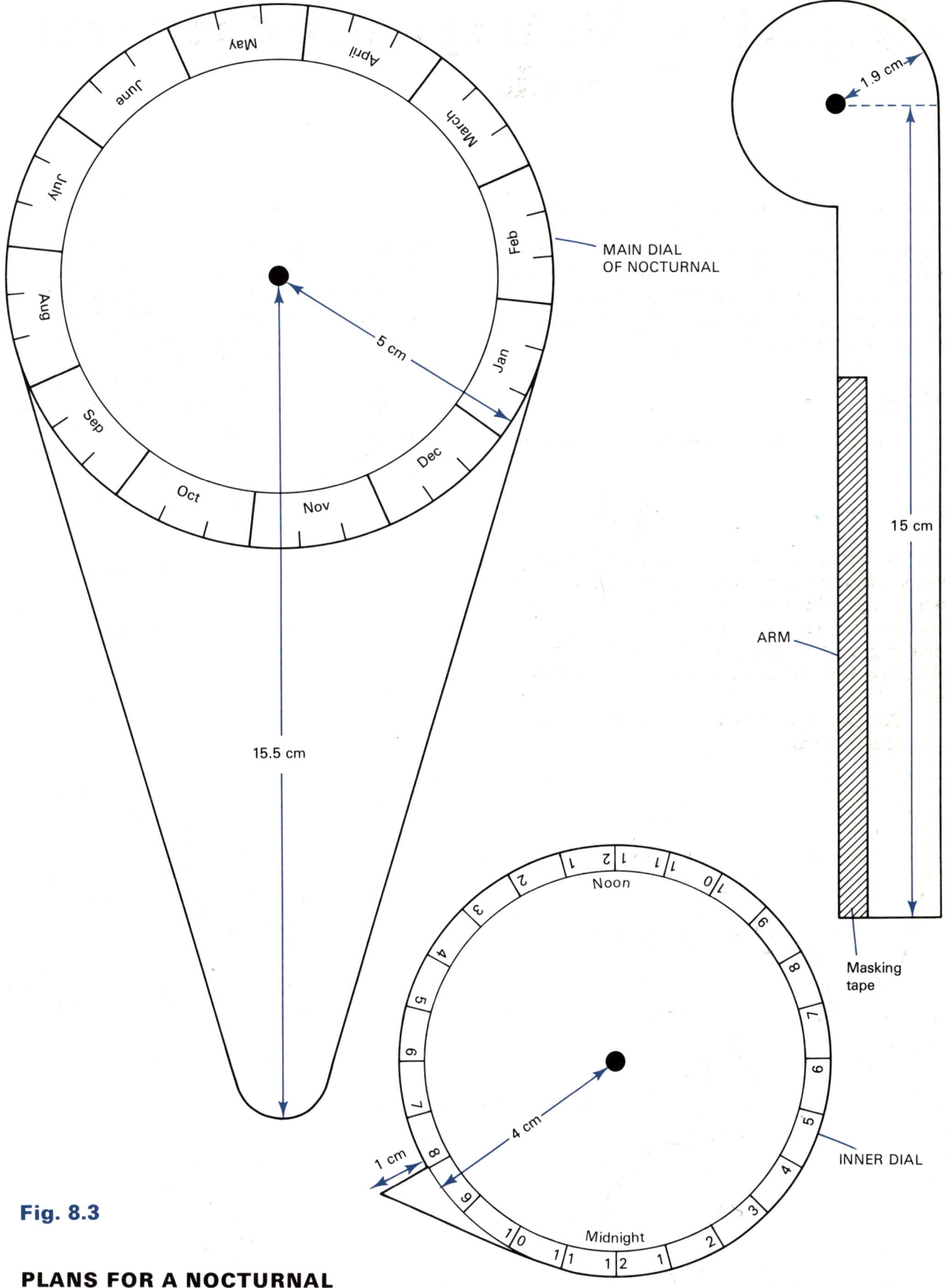

MAIN DIAL
OF NOCTURNAL

5 cm

15.5 cm

ARM

15 cm

1.9 cm.

Masking
tape

INNER DIAL

4 cm

1 cm

Noon

Midnight

Fig. 8.3

PLANS FOR A NOCTURNAL

PROJECT 9 The seasonal constellations

Circumpolar stars are seen all the year round. There are other constellations that we only see during certain seasons of the year. In this project we learn how to find some of these constellations. The descriptions given here refer to the seasonal star maps given at the front and back of this book.

1 The winter constellations

We will start with the winter sky because it contains many bright stars and several constellations that are easy to find. The three stars that form the belt of Orion the Hunter are very easy to identify as they are almost equally bright and in a straight line. These stars are sometimes called the Three Kings. They are surrounded by a rectangle standing on one of its shorter sides, which forms the body of Orion. The star map of the winter constellations, together with fig. 9.1, should help you recognise Orion. If you extend the imaginary line joining the Three Kings out to your left, then slightly below this line you will see the brightest star in the sky – Sirius, or the Dog Star. It is so called because it is supposed to be in the head of Orion's larger dog, Canis Major. If you take your same imaginary line out to your right, slightly above the line you will see a reddish star called Aldebaran, which is one of the eyes of Taurus the Bull. Using the chart of Orion, together with the star map, see if you can find some of the other stars and constellations.

2 The spring constellations

As we have seen, the Plough is part of the constellation of Ursa Major (or the Great Bear).

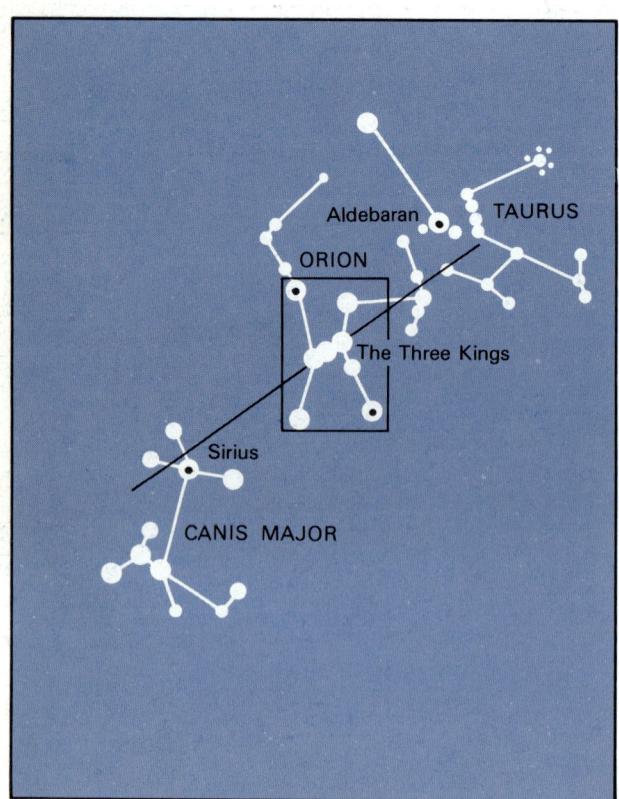

Fig. 9.1 Star chart corresponding to star map of Winter Constellations

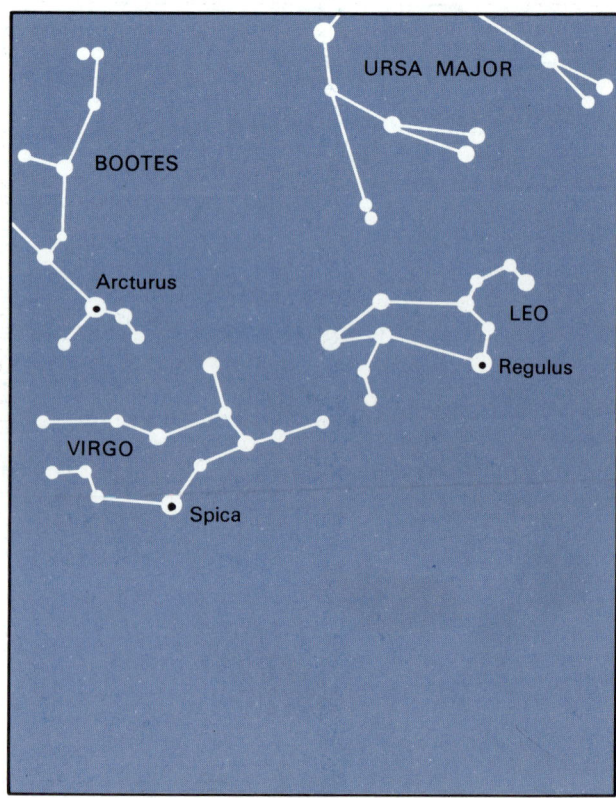

Fig. 9.2 Star chart corresponding to star map of Spring Constellations

At the top of this star map you will see the legs of Ursa Major. Just below the back legs you will find the constellation of Leo the Lion. At this time of year Ursa Major is very high in the sky and Leo will be south of it. He can be identified by the back-to-front question mark that forms his mane. Regulus is the brightest star in Leo, see fig. 9.2. To the left of Leo and slightly lower in the sky is the constellation of Virgo the Virgin. The brightest star in this constellation is Spica. Slightly above and to the left of Spica (see fig. 9.2) you come to a rather bright star called Arcturus, which is the brightest star in the constellation of Bootes, or the Herdsman. The three stars Spica, Arcturus and Regulus form a triangle in the spring sky that can be useful in identifying other constellations as shown on the map of spring constellations.

3 The summer constellations

The summer sky is dominated by a very large triangle called the Summer Triangle. It rises in the east in the early evening, is almost directly overhead at about midnight, and just before sunrise can be seen in the western sky. Each of its three stars, however, belongs to a different constellation, as you can see from fig. 9.3. Deneb is in the tail of Cygnus the Swan; Vega is in the constellation of Lyra; Altair is in Aquila the Eagle. On a clear night away from city lights, you can see passing through the Summer Triangle an important part of the Milky Way. This, you will remember, is the name of our galaxy. To the east of the Summer Triangle can be seen the rather small and faint constellation of Delphinus the Dolphin.

4 The autumn constellations

The most prominent feature of the autumn sky is the Great Square of Pegasus as shown in fig. 9.4. Pegasus (the Flying Horse) is seen upside down if you are looking up facing towards the south part of the sky. To the east of Pegasus is the constellation of Andromeda. An imaginary straight line drawn from the two most westerly stars of the Square of Pegasus will also take you to Polaris.

All the descriptions given here should help you find the most important constellations to be seen at different times of year. Once you have learned these constellations you can use them to find the less well-known ones.

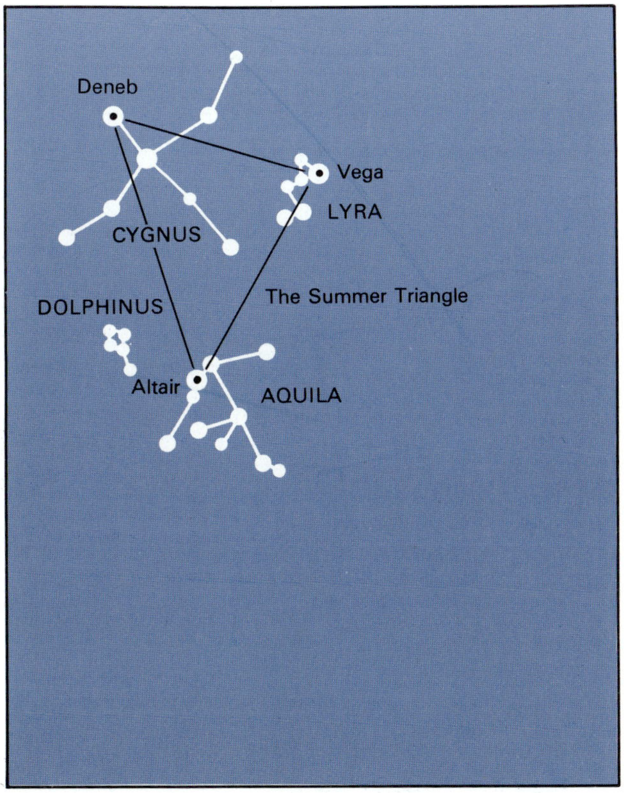

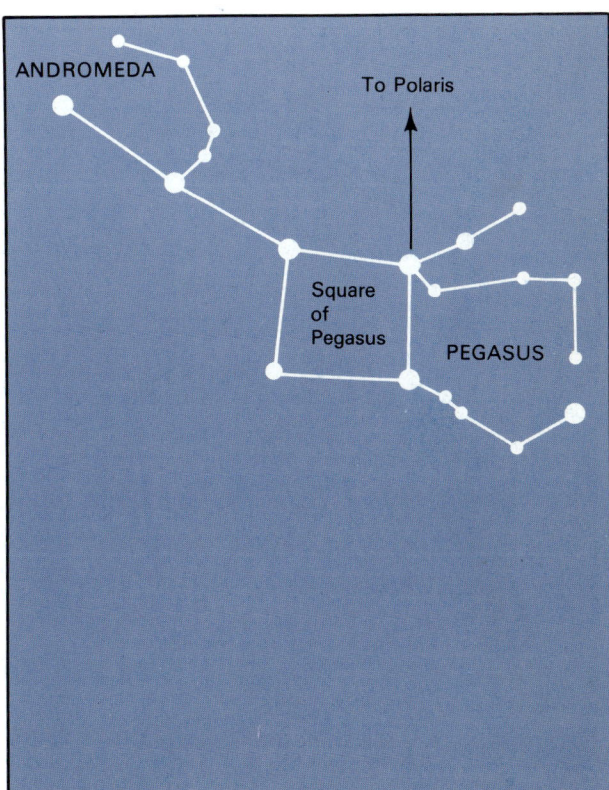

Fig. 9.3 Star chart corresponding to star map of Summer Constellations

Fig. 9.4 Star chart corresponding to star map Autumn Constellations

PROJECT 10 Making and using a simple planisphere

A *planisphere* is used to find which constellations are visible on any night at any time. Using the following instructions, make yourself a planisphere and then go out on a clear night to try it out. Note, a planisphere is not really a star map, but a device to help you find which constellations are visible on a particular night. It shows only the more important stars in each constellation and as a result the shapes of the constellations differ slightly from those shown on the star maps. You will find that constellations are often drawn differently on different maps: do not worry about this because there is really no 'correct' way to draw any constellation.

What you need

Stiff white paper or thin card; acetate or celluloid sheet; brass paper fastener; glue.

What to do

1 Trace star map shown in fig. 10.2 onto stiff paper or thin card and cut out.

2 Trace circular window frame shown in fig. 10.3 on to white card and cut out. Carefully cut out shaded area.

3 Draw circle of same diameter as window frame onto acetate sheet and cut out.

4 Glue window frame to acetate circle to make window. Place window over top of star map so that centres coincide and with a sharp point make holes through centres of both. Join with brass paper fastener as shown in fig. 10.1.

The *Daily Telegraph* produces a circular star map which may be used to make a larger planisphere. Instructions on how to do this accompany the map. Other commercially produced planispheres are also available fairly cheaply from bookshops.

Using the planisphere

To find which constellations are visible at a given time of night on a particular date, line up the time on the window frame with date on the star map (this will have to be an estimate since this planisphere is too small to show days of the month). The constellations visible that night will be those showing through the clear part of the window. To find the direction and position of stars in the real sky, hold the planisphere facing downwards above your head. Now point the midnight mark towards north and the noon mark towards south. The eastern and western horizons are marked at the edge of the clear window. The position of constellations on the map which appear in the window will be very similar to their positions in the actual sky.

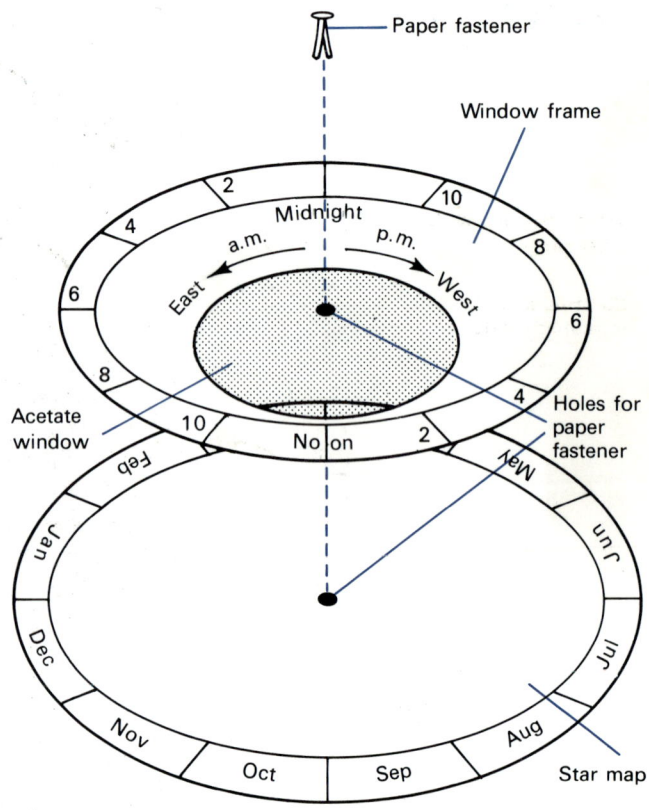

Fig. 10.1

PLANS FOR A PLANISPHERE

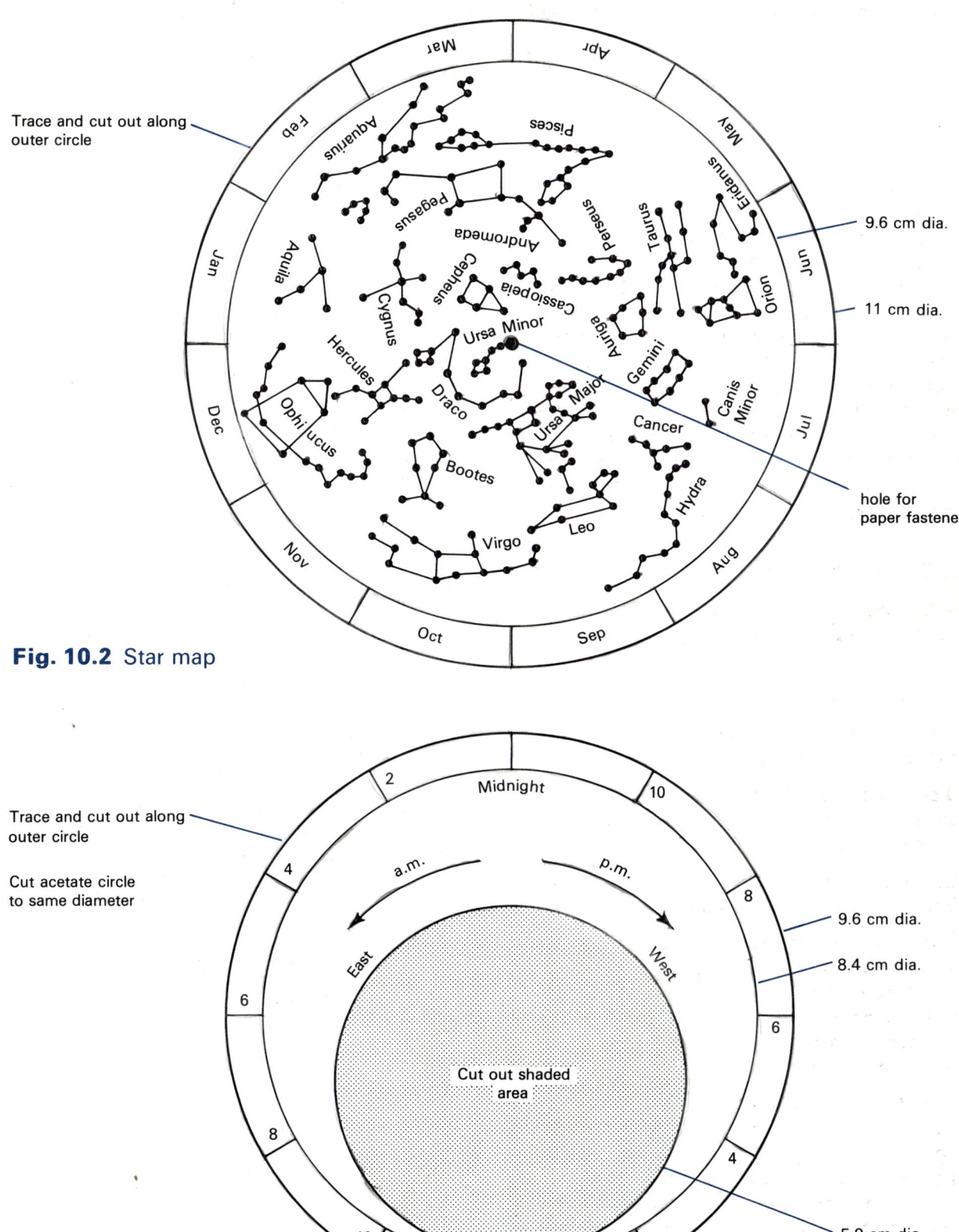

Trace and cut out along outer circle

9.6 cm dia.

11 cm dia.

hole for paper fastener

Fig. 10.2 Star map

Trace and cut out along outer circle

Cut acetate circle to same diameter

9.6 cm dia.

8.4 cm dia.

5.9 cm dia.

Midnight

a.m.   p.m.

East   West

Cut out shaded area

Noon

Fig. 10.3 Window frame

PROJECT 11 Finding out about the motion and phases of the Moon

It is possible to make maps of positions of the stars because, as seen from the Earth, they do not change their distances from each other over long periods of time. The Moon, however, changes position against the stars both as the month goes by and also as the year passes. We say the Moon has phases because we see different parts of the Moon lit up by the light from the Sun as the month goes by. In this project we see how the Moon moves among the stars and how it phases as it does so. This project takes about one month to complete.

What you need

Copies of the star map provided in Project 9; small table; torch; piece of red cloth; elastic band; two transparent plastic rulers about 30 cm long; piece of wood 50 cm long, 2 cm diameter (part of old broom-handle will do); No. 8 screw 1.5 cm long; brace fitted with No. 8 bit; drill.

What to do

1 Drill a hole in the centre of one of the rulers.

2 Drill a hole in the end of piece of wood, and screw ruler to wood as shown in fig. 11.1. This is called a 'forestaff'.

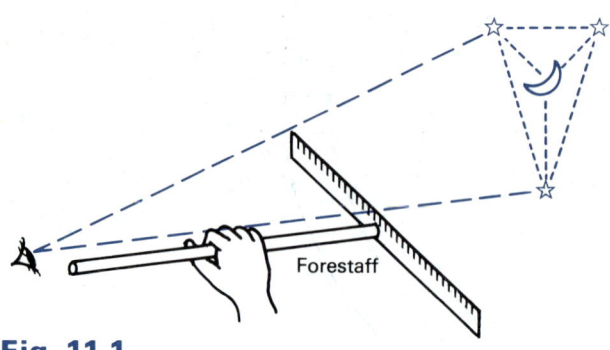

Fig. 11.1

3 Cover torch light with red cloth and hold in place with elastic band.

4 Choose the star map appropriate to the time of year.

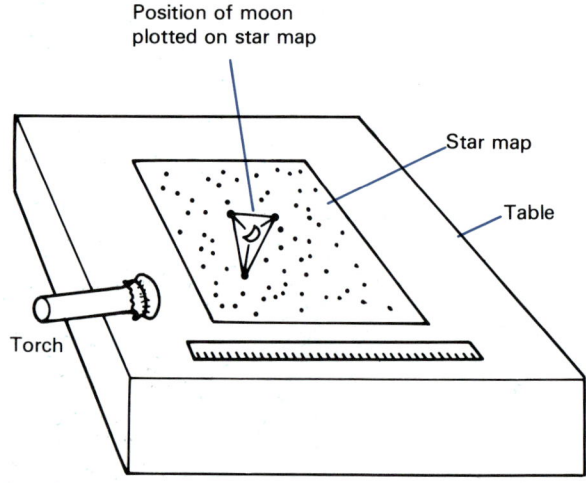

Fig. 11.2

5 Set up a table outside on a clear night when the moon is visible and with a good view of the sky. Place the map on the table. The torch is to help you see what you are doing without disturbing your view of the night sky (see fig. 11.2).

6 Observe which constellation the Moon is in. Using the forestaff, measure the distances from each other of any of the three brightest stars in the constellation. Also measure the distance of the Moon from these stars as shown in fig. 11.1.

7 Using simple proportions, transfer this information to the star map and so plot the position of the Moon on the map.

8 Note how much of the Moon's disc is visible and record this, together with the date, on your map.

9 Repeat these observations on as many days as possible for about 28 days, starting on a date 2–3 days after New Moon. (The Moon is not visible when quite new: this is because it is in the same general direction as the Sun, and the dark side is facing the Earth.) *Note*: you may have to use more than one of your star maps during this period.

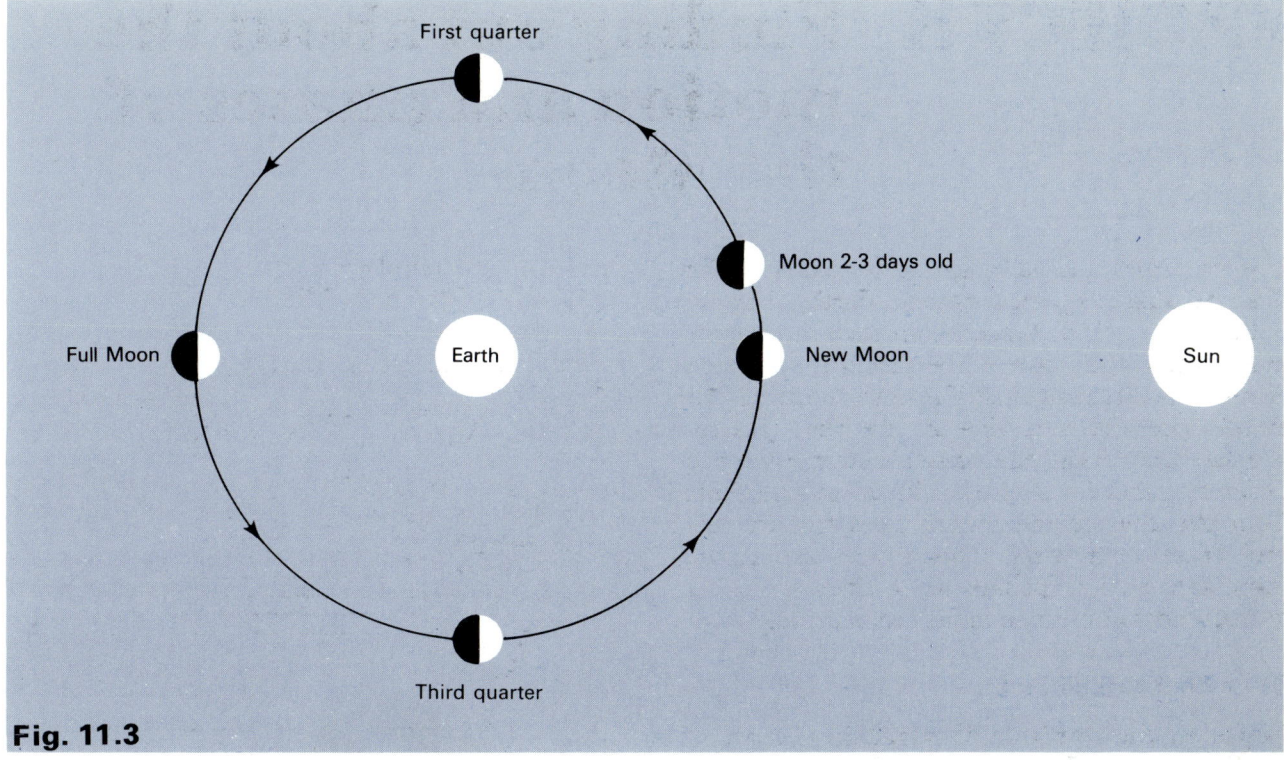

Fig. 11.3

From your observations you will notice that when the Moon is 2–3 days old only a thin crescent is lit up, and it is very low in the western sky. After four or five days the Moon reaches what we call the First Quarter, when half of its face is lit up and it is seen towards the south. Seven days later the Moon will be full, the whole of its face will be lit up, and it will be seen rising towards the east just after sunset. Seven days after this the Moon will only rise at about midnight, and the half of its face towards the eastern horizon will be lit up. This phase is known as the Third Quarter. The four phases are therefore New Moon; First Quarter; Full Moon; and Third Quarter.

In the northern hemisphere the Moon is always south of the Zenith when it reaches its greatest altitude.

These naked eye observations of the Moon are an important start to the telescopic observations which will be one of our later projects.

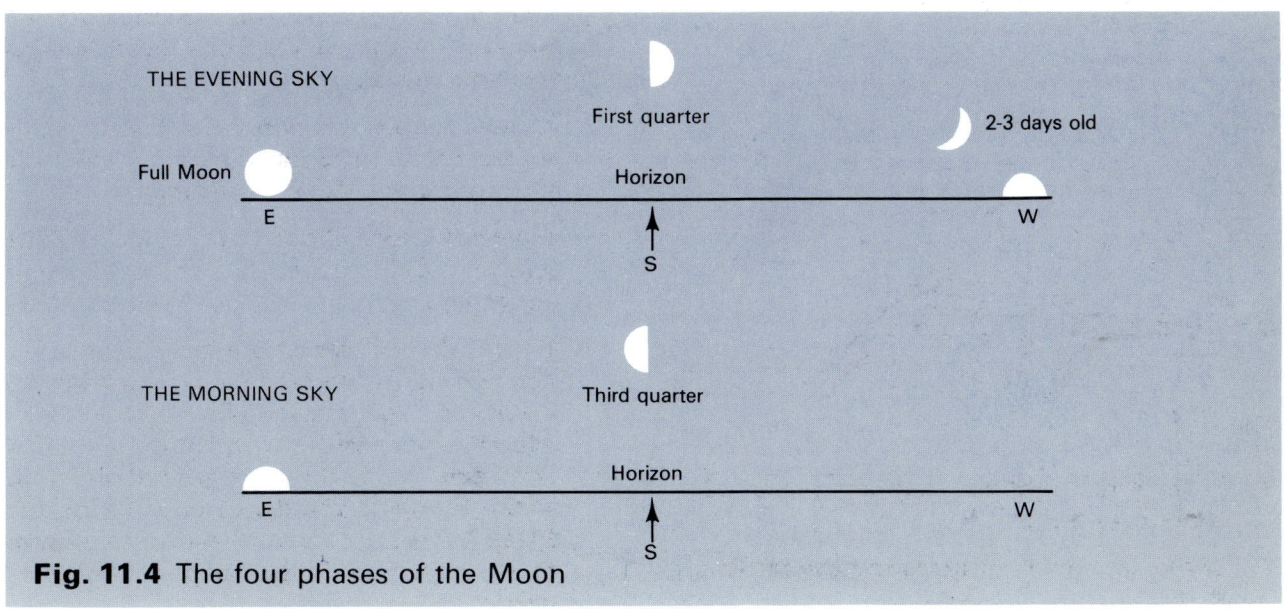

Fig. 11.4 The four phases of the Moon

PROJECT 12 Finding out about the motion of the planets

The planets look like stars, but they change their position against the stars. In addition to taking part in the general east-west motion of most of the stars they also move very slightly with respect to the stars in the course of one night. With some of the planets this motion is noticeable after several days, with others only after a few weeks, even in some cases after a few months. There are eight major planets visible from the Earth with a telescope: five of these can be seen with the naked eye. These are Mercury, Venus, Mars, Jupiter and Saturn. Mercury is rather hard to see because it never gets very far from the Sun in the sky and quite often is lost in the morning or evening glow. For this reason we will leave it out of this project. This is really a long-term project and, while some of the ideas will emerge if you continue your observations for several months, you would learn a great deal more by continuing for a few years.

What you need

Flashlight battery, bulb and bulb-holder; 40 cm copper wire with PVC insulation; shoebox with lid; sheet of perspex big enough to fit lid of box; felt-tip pens; tracing paper; sellotape; small hand-saw; tracing paper copies of the star maps given in Project 9; forestaff made in Project 11. You will also need planetary charts showing positions of the planets for each month, and these are obtainable from the national papers each month or can be bought from booksellers (see Appendix 4).

What to do

This project uses the same method as Project 11 to plot the changing positions of planets against the background stars, but using tracing paper copies of the star maps placed on top of a simple light box.

1   Cut rectangular hole in box lid leaving 2 cm border around edge, as shown in fig. 12.1a.

2   Saw perspex sheet to size of box lid and glue to border.

3   Glue a piece of clean tracing paper to underside of lid (this will help to diffuse light), as shown in fig. 12.1b.

4   Connect battery to bulb-holder with copper wire and sellotape battery, bulb-holder and wire to inside bottom of box. Screw bulb into place (see fig. 12.1c and d). Bulb is switched on by connnecting wire to terminals.

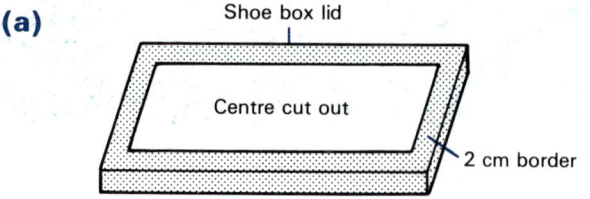

(a) Shoe box lid / Centre cut out / 2 cm border

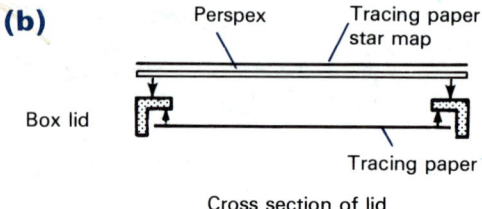

(b) Perspex / Tracing paper star map / Box lid / Tracing paper

Cross section of lid

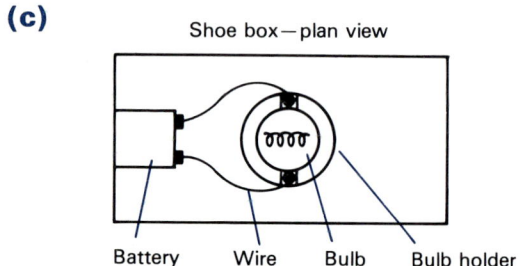

(c) Shoe box—plan view / Battery / Wire / Bulb / Bulb holder

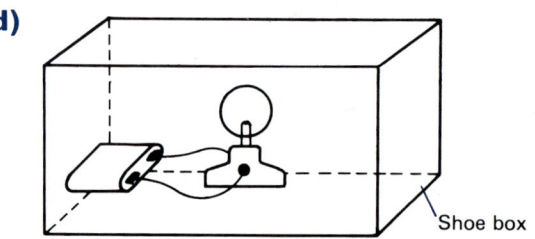

(d) Shoe box

Fig. 12.1

Plotting the planets

Planetary charts are simplified diagrams showing only the most conspicuous stars, and you would not expect consistency with star maps. The planetary charts in this book are similar to those found in some magazines and newspapers. They show positions of the five 'naked-eye' planets on a given date with respect to the brighter stars in the constellations. This helps you to know where to look in a given constellation for a particular planet (see fig. 12.2).

Plot each planet on tracing paper star map using a different colour pen for each planet. As the planets move with differing speeds against the background stars it is not necessary to plot each planet every time you make an observation. Venus can be plotted once or twice a week; Mars once a week; Jupiter and Saturn only about twice a month. Use the monthly planetary charts to tell you more or less where to find the planets, but try to find the actual positions from your own observations of the night sky. The charts usually give planetary positions for the beginning, middle and end of each month, and these will not be exactly the same as the positions on the nights that you make your observations.

From your observations you should be able to see that the planets move with different speeds against the background stars, and should be able to arrange the planets in order of speed. You may also notice that each planet varies its own speed and sometimes seems to stand still. Its direction also changes, and sometimes it will seem to move backwards against the stars for a short period (see Appendix 5 for a brief explanation of planetary motion).

Once we have learned more about lenses and how to make telescopes, it will be possible to observe the planets through telescopes, but these naked-eye observations are useful in identifying planets and knowing where to look for them.

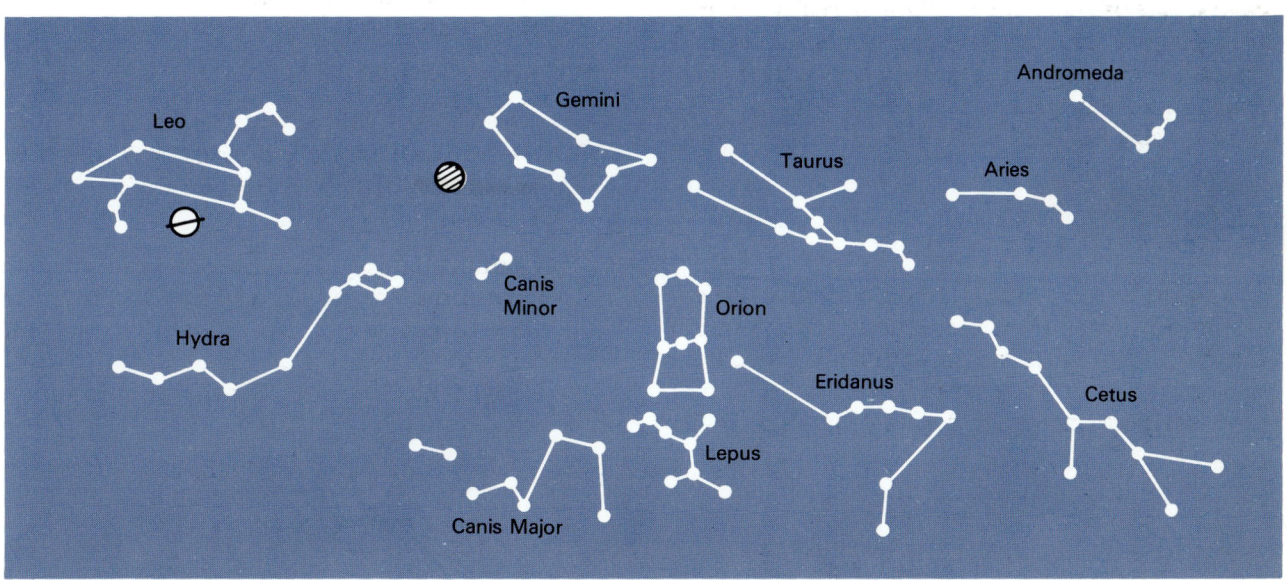

Fig. 12.2 Planet chart of Saturn (♄) and Jupiter (♃) for February, 1979

PROJECT 13 Introduction to lenses and telescopes

This information will be helpful for later projects on making telescopes.

WARNING: Never look at the Sun through a lens, telescope or pair of binoculars, or even directly. If you do, you will almost certainly damage your eyes permanently.

Beams and rays of light

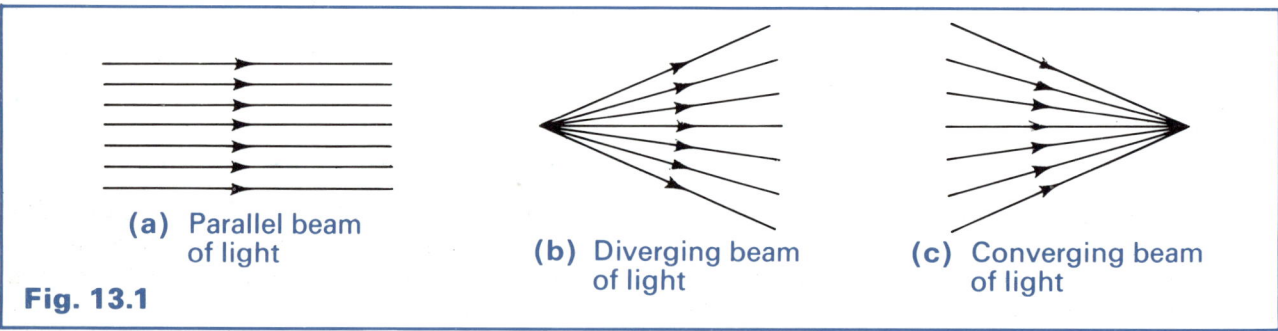

(a) Parallel beam of light

(b) Diverging beam of light

(c) Converging beam of light

Fig. 13.1

Beams of light consist of a large number of individual rays and each ray can be treated as a straight line. A parallel beam thus consists of many parallel rays of light as shown in fig. 13.1a.

A diverging beam is one in which the distances get progressively larger, while in the converging beam the distances get progressively smaller (see fig. 13.1b and c).

Lenses

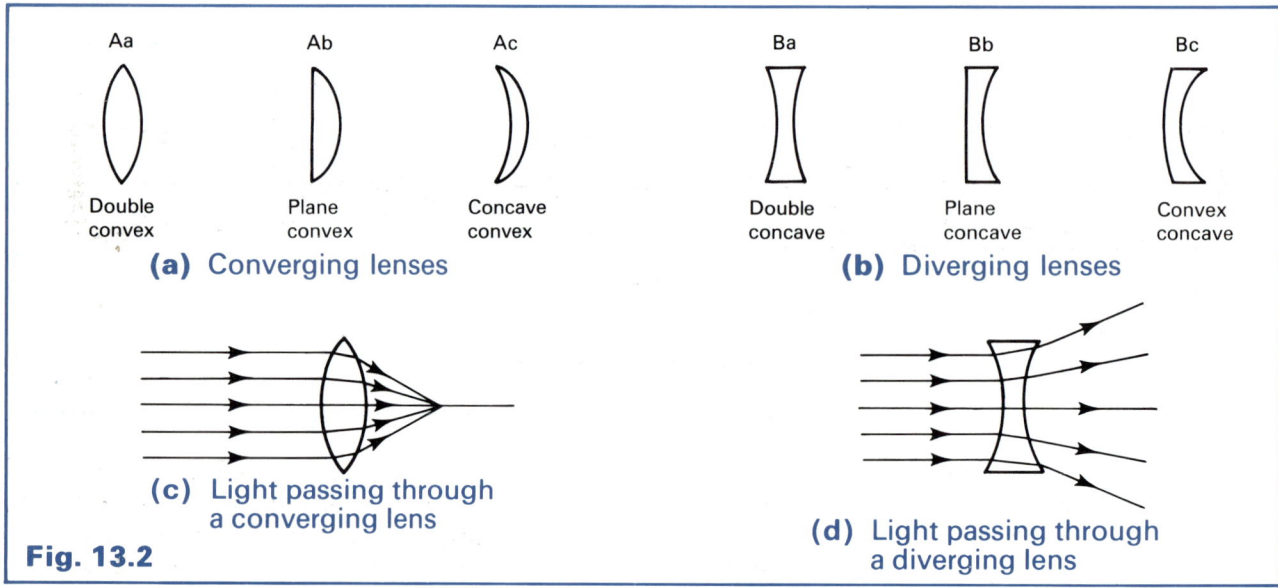

Aa — Double convex

Ab — Plane convex

Ac — Concave convex

(a) Converging lenses

Ba — Double concave

Bb — Plane concave

Bc — Convex concave

(b) Diverging lenses

(c) Light passing through a converging lens

(d) Light passing through a diverging lens

Fig. 13.2

The main property of a lens is that it will bend a ray of light. Lenses come in a variety of shapes and sizes but are classified into two main groups depending on how they affect a parallel beam of light, i.e. converging (fig. 13.2a) or diverging (fig. 13.2b). Figs. 13.2c and d show how a typical member of each group affects a parallel beam of light.

Converging lenses

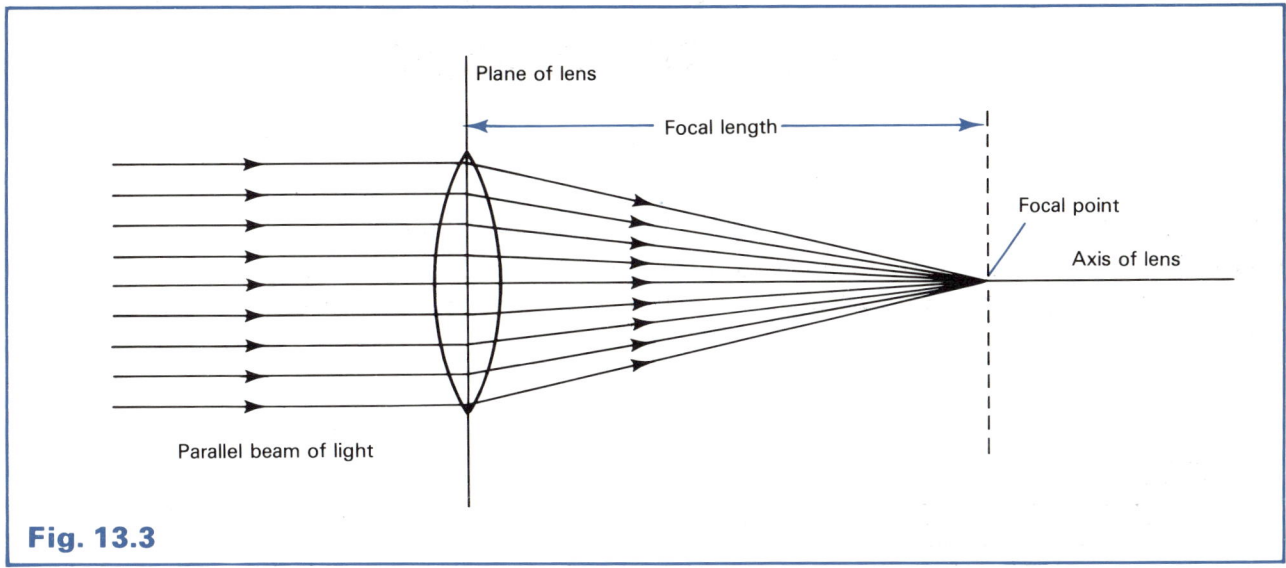

Fig. 13.3

These are the lenses most often used in telescopes so we will concentrate on these. The plane passing through the circumference and centre of a double convex lens is called the 'plane of the lens' (fig. 13.3) and the line at right angles to this and passing through the centre is called the 'axis of the lens'. The point at which a parallel beam (parallel to the axis) is focussed after passing through the lens is called the *focal point*. The distance of the focal point from the plane of the lens is called the *focal length*. The shorter the focal length, the higher the magnification of the lens, so a short focal length lens is said to be more powerful than a long focal length lens.

Light from distant objects (e.g. the Sun) is travelling in very nearly parallel beams when it reaches the Earth. We can thus use it to find the focal length of a converging lens, by focussing an image of the Sun onto a sheet of card and then measuring the distance between lens and card.

Formation of images by a converging lens

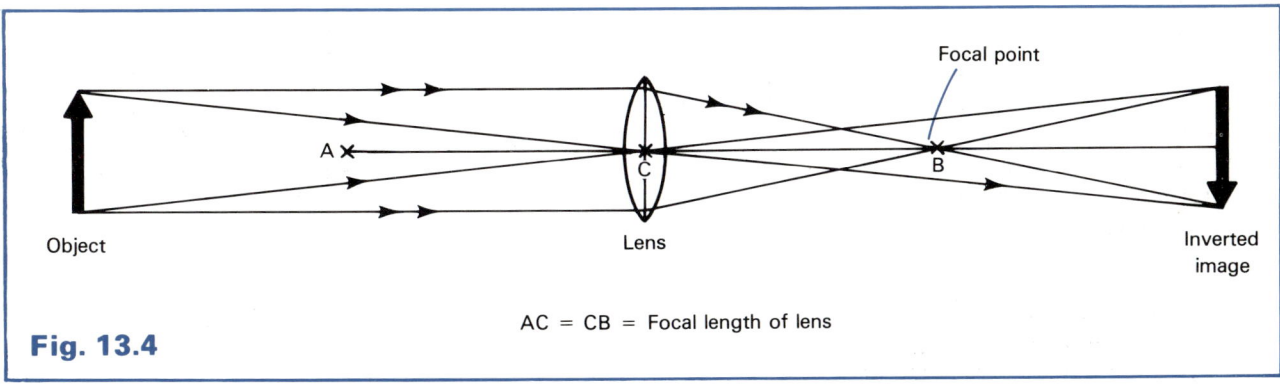

AC = CB = Focal length of lens

Fig. 13.4

We can now see how a converging lens forms an image. Any ray parallel to the axis of the lens which passes through the lens will be bent to pass through the focal point. Only rays passing through the centre of the lens will not be bent. Provided the distance between any object and the lens is greater than the focal length of the lens, an image of the object can be focussed on a screen, as shown in fig. 13.4. Such an image is called a *real image* and it will be inverted. If the distance between object and lens is less than the focal length of the lens the image cannot be focussed on a screen, but the eye will see an enlarged image of the object on looking through the lens, as shown in fig. 13.5. In this case the image will be seen upright, and is called a *virtual image*.

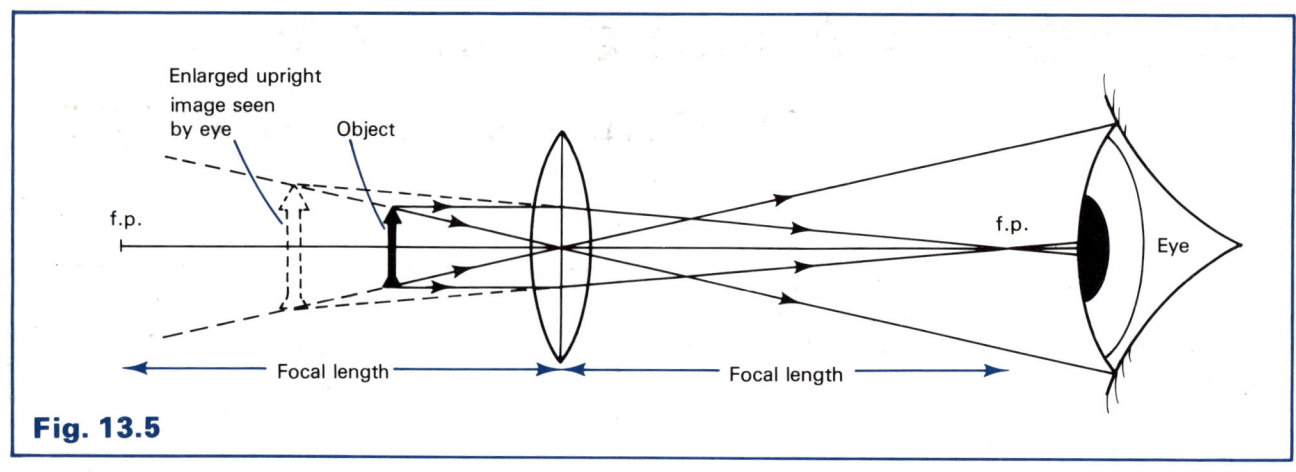

Fig. 13.5

The astronomical telescope

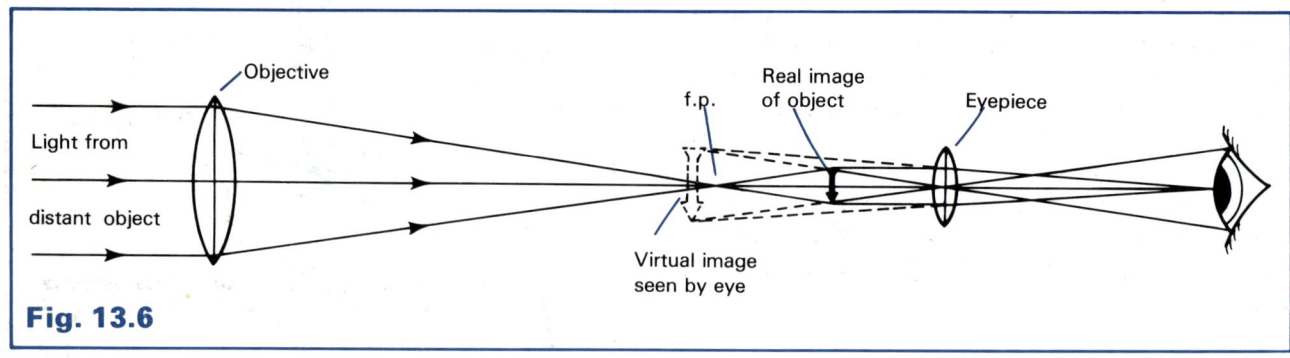

Fig. 13.6

This telescope consists of two converging lenses. The lens at the front is called the *objective* and it collects the light from the object being observed and forms a real (inverted) image of the object within the telescope. The second lens at the other end of the telescope is called the *eyepiece* and this gives the observer an enlarged virtual image. However, as the first image of the object formed by the objective was inverted the virtual image will also be inverted (see fig. 13.6).

The *magnification* of the telescope (its power to enlarge images) is calculated as follows:

$$\text{Magnification} = \frac{\text{Focal length of objective}}{\text{Focal length of eyepiece}}$$

PROJECT 14 Making a simple astronomical telescope

In this project we make a simple astronomical telescope out of readily available materials. Again you will need a fairly large room for this project.

What you need

(Dimensions are approximate)
1 converging lens 70 cm focal length, 4 cm diameter; 1 converging lens 3 cm focal length, 4 cm diameter; cardboard tube, length 60 cm, outer diameter 3 cm; another card tube able to slide easily but not freely within first tube, length 20 cm; block of wood 10 cm × 6 cm × 1 cm; 2 blocks of wood 1 cm × 6 cm × 5 cm; thin card (to make flanges); camera tripod stand; 2 rubber bands about 22 cm long, 0.6 cm wide; keyhole saw; screws; metre stick; plasticine; tracing paper.

Understanding the astronomical telescope

This experiment will show you the principle of an astronomical telescope.

1   Set up a metre stick on a small table opposite a window so that the end of the stick nearer the window is at least 3 metres from the window, as shown in fig. 14.1.

2   Attach long focal length lens (about 70 cm) with plasticine at right angles to one end of metre stick as shown.

3   Hold tracing paper at right angles to metre stick and move it back and forth until you get an inverted view of the window.

4   Take short focal length lens and move it back and forth along other end of metre stick until your eye can see an enlarged view of the inverted image on the tracing paper through the lens.

5   Attach short focal length lens to metre stick at this point with plasticine, and remove tracing paper. You will still see the image but brighter and clearer. Now you are ready to make your astronomical telescope.

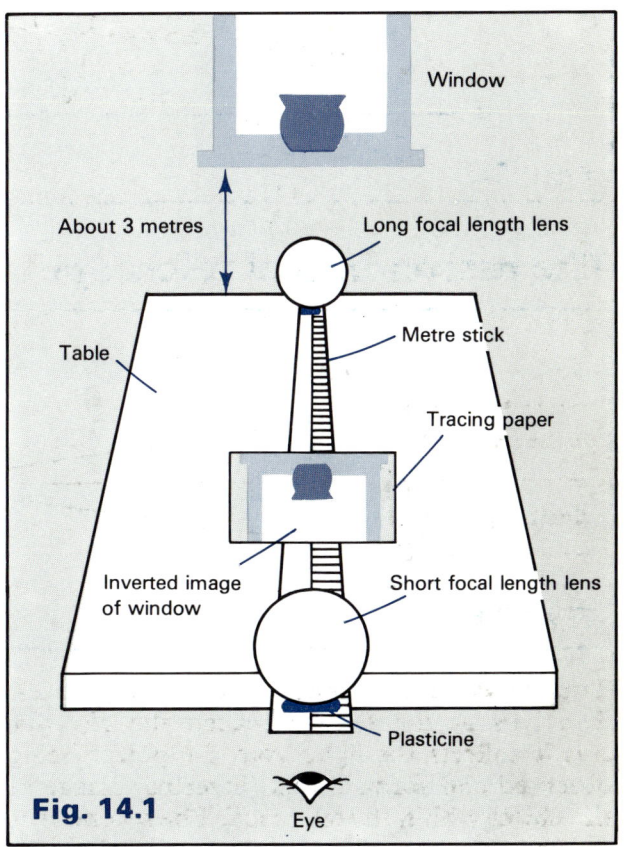

Fig. 14.1

Making the telescope

1   Make two card flanges to fit around each tube, as shown in figs. 14.2a and b.

2   Glue flanges to ends of tubes leaving lugs free and bent back at right angles.

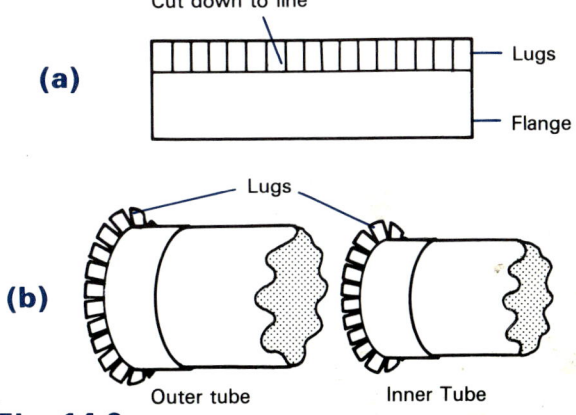

Fig. 14.2

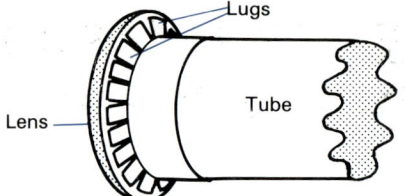

Fig. 14.3

Lugs
Lens
Tube

3 Glue long focal length lens (objective) to lugs on larger tube, and short focal length lens (eyepiece) to lugs on smaller tube as shown in fig. 14.3.

4 Slide smaller tube into larger.

5 Saw semi-circle 3 cm diameter into each of two pieces of wood 1 cm × 6 cm × 5 cm, as shown in fig. 14.4.

6 Screw these pieces of wood to third piece as shown in fig. 14.5.

7 Screw base of telescope cradle to top of camera tripod stand, place telescope in cradle and attach with elastic bands (see fig. 14.6).

Try out your telescope on some distant objects to begin with. You focus it by sliding the thinner tube in or out until you get a clear image. Remember, in this telescope the image will be inverted.

Fig. 14.4

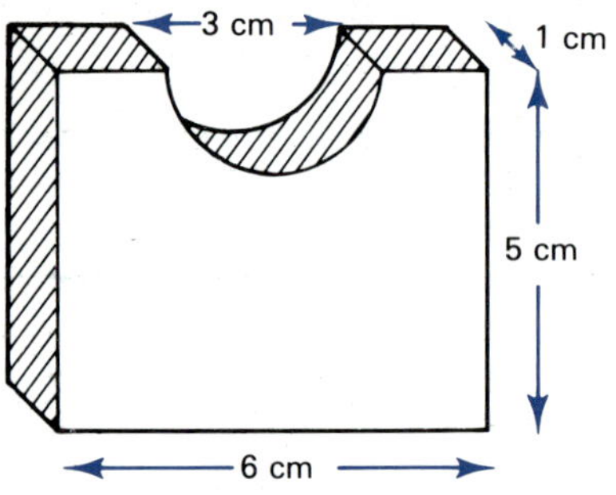

3 cm
1 cm
5 cm
6 cm

Fig. 14.5

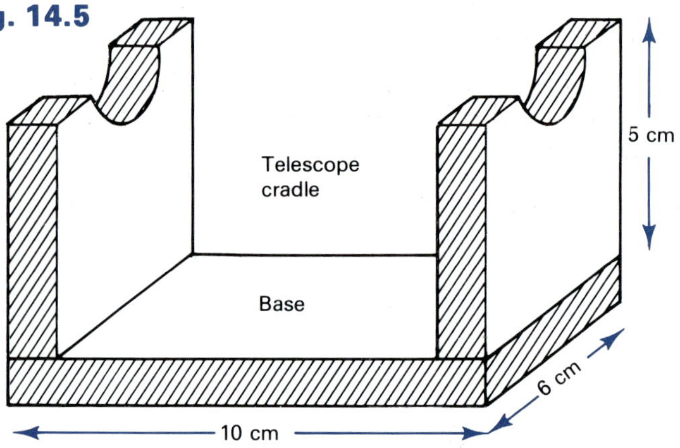

Telescope cradle
Base
5 cm
6 cm
10 cm

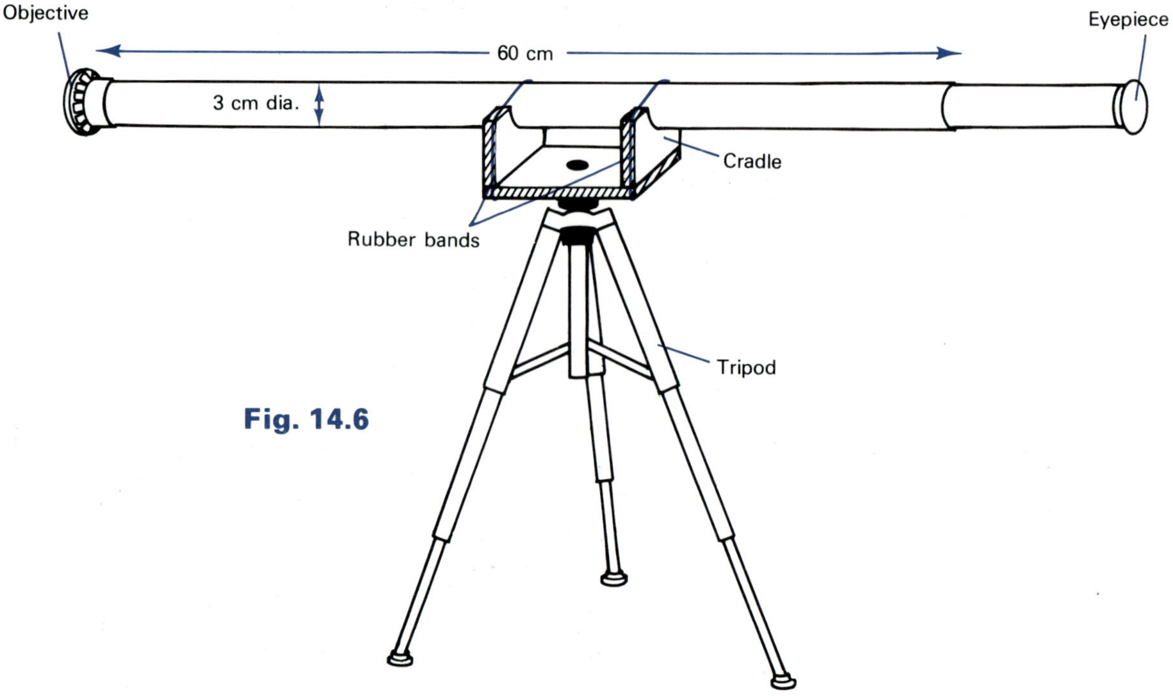

Objective
60 cm
3 cm dia.
Eyepiece
Cradle
Rubber bands
Tripod

Fig. 14.6

PROJECT 15 Using your telescope to study the Sun

WARNING: Never look through this telescope at the Sun: you would permanently damage your eyes.

What you need

Telescope made in Project 14; stiff copper wire; thin wire; 2 sheets of stiff white card about 13 × 13 cm; 3 drawing pins; sellotape.

What to do

We cannot look directly at the Sun, but we can project an image of it onto a screen.

1   Cut hole equal in diameter to outer diameter of larger tube, in centre of one sheet of card, as shown in fig. 15.1*a*.

2   Slip card over back end of larger tube and use three drawing pins to fix it to back of cradle (see fig. 15.1*b*). This screen will prevent direct sunlight from reaching projection screen. Call this screen A.

3   Make a wire cage to support projection screen B as shown in fig. 15.1*c*. Bend corners around a block of wood and use thinner wire to join sections together.

4   Sellotape screen B (other piece of card) to wire cage as shown in fig. 15.1*d*.

5   Sellotape wire cage to eyepiece tube as shown in fig. 15.1*e*.

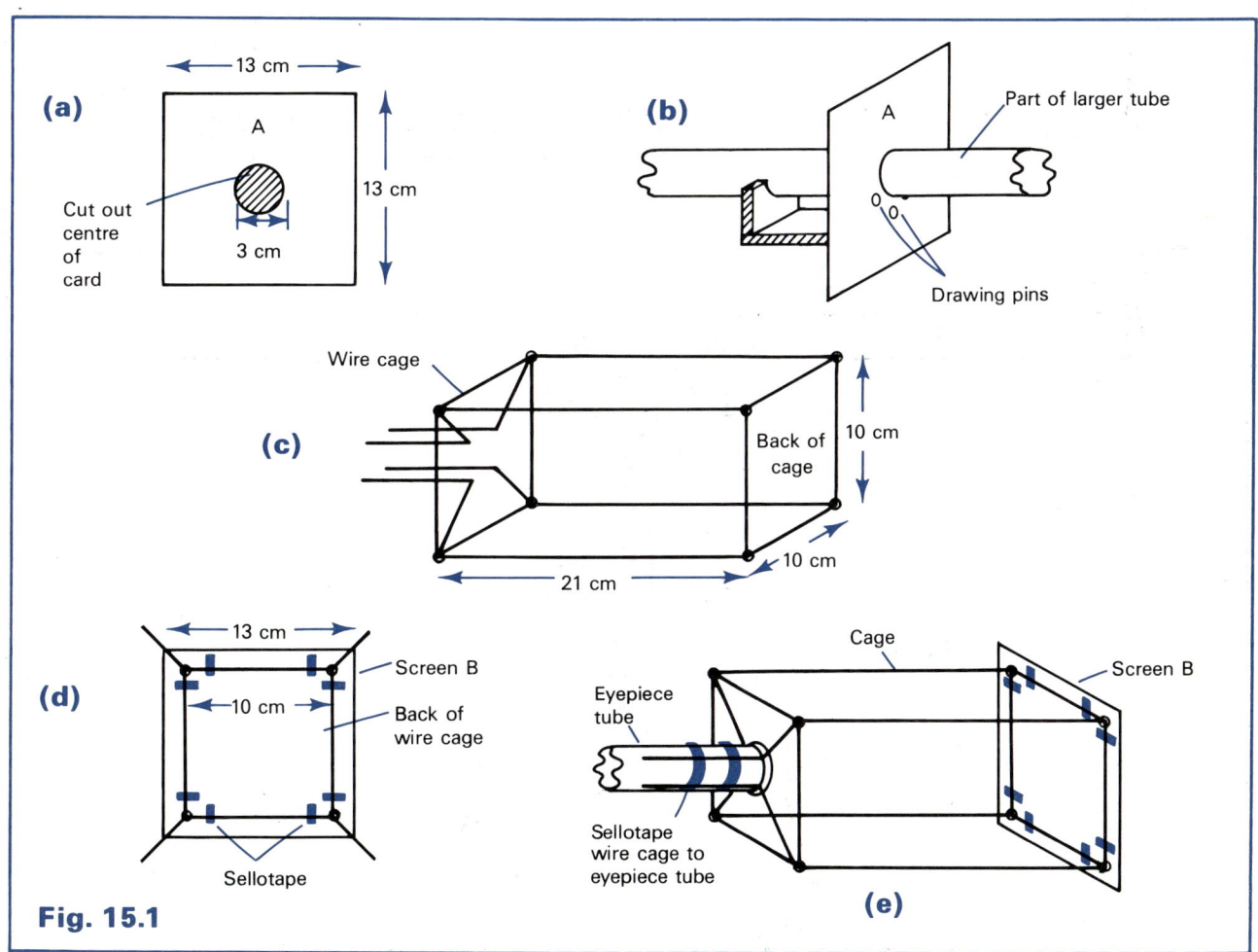

Fig. 15.1

6 Slide eyepiece tube into objective tube.

7 Adjust telescope on tripod until shadow of screen A covers whole of projection screen B. There will now be a circle of light in centre of projection screen, as shown in fig. 15.2.

8 Slide eyepiece tube in and out until you get an enlarged image of the Sun on projection screen. This happens when the overall distance between objective lens and eyepiece lens is about 0.5 cm or more greater than the sum of their focal lengths.

You can now begin your study of the Sun.

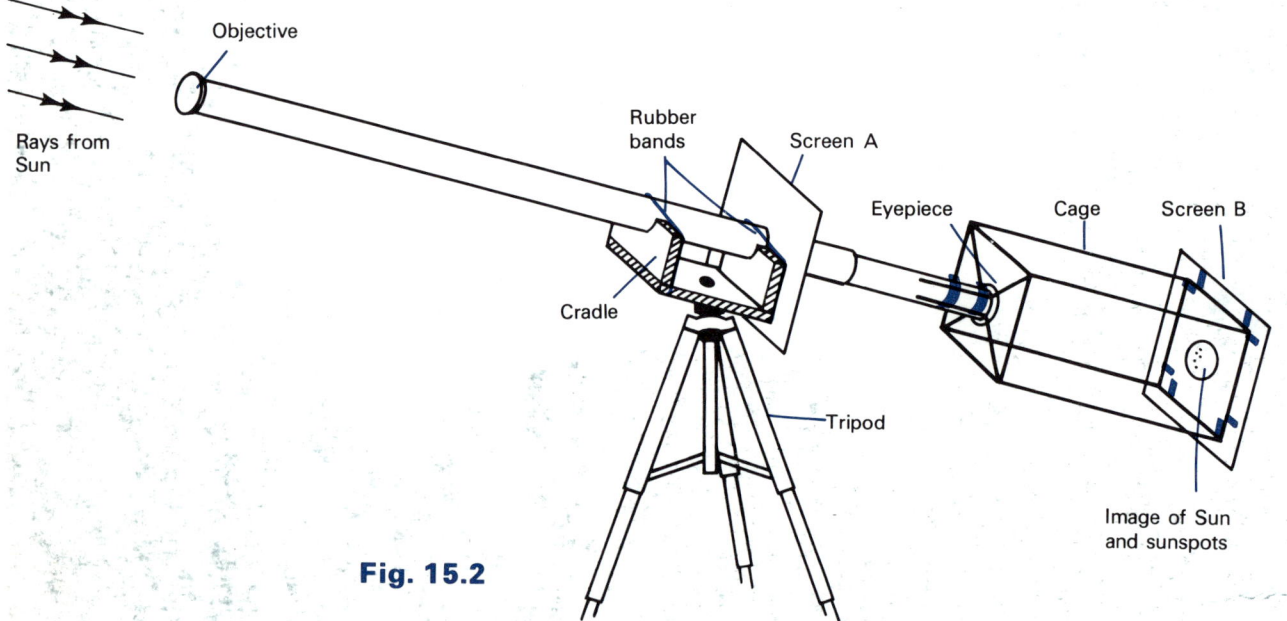

Fig. 15.2

Sunspots

Sunspots are parts of the Sun that are cooler than the rest of the surface, so they appear as black spots against the bright disc of the Sun. Sometimes they occur singly, but more often in pairs and sometimes they are parts of large groups of sunspots.

The Sun's surface frequently has at least a few sunspots which can be seen on a projected image with this telescope. Mark the positions of any sunspots you can see on your screen. Repeat observations once a day over the next few days. After a few days you may notice that the spots seem to move across the disc of the Sun, which shows that the Sun is spinning on its own axis. You could follow a group of sunspots across the disc, see them disappear at one edge, and wait for a few days to see if they will reappear at the opposite edge. You could also count the number of sunspots that you can see on a given day. If you were to extend your observations over several years you would notice that in some years there are many more sunspots than in other

years. Some scientists claim that these sunspots affect long term climate, and also our own short term weather.

Eclipses

Eclipses of the Sun by the Moon only happen rarely at any one point on the surface of the Earth. An eclipse of the Sun occurs when the Moon is somewhere between us and the Sun, thus casting a shadow on some parts of the Earth (see fig. 15.3). To observe an eclipse you need

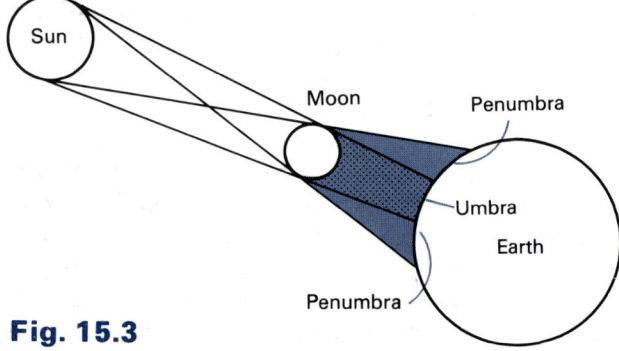

Fig. 15.3

Fig. 15.4a Partial eclipse of Sun

to know rather precisely when it is going to occur and whether you are likely to see it from where you live. You can find this information in the *Nautical Almanac* (which you could look at in your local library) or in the *Handbook of the British Astronomical Association*. Set up your telescope to point to the Sun a few minutes before the eclipse is due to start. You will have to move the telescope to keep the Sun in view, because the Sun will seem to be moving across the sky (due to the spinning of the Earth). As the eclipse begins you will notice a slight 'bite' being taken out of the Sun. This 'bite' (see fig. 15.4*a*) will grow as the eclipse progresses, and if the eclipse is total (very rare) the whole disc will gradually disappear from your screen. It will reappear a few seconds later, and the 'bite' will get smaller and smaller again.

You might be lucky enough to witness an *annular eclipse*, also a very rare event. The Moon covers the Sun's disc as in a total eclipse, but because of the slight changes in their distances from the Earth, the Sun's disc appears to be slightly larger than the Moon. As a result the Moon does not completely blot out the Sun and

Fig. 15.4b Total eclipse of Sun

the Sun appears as a thin ring, or *annulus*.

An eclipse may be seen as total on one part of the Earth's surface, and as partial elsewhere on the same occasion. The shadow cast by the Moon is divided into two regions (see fig. 15.3). The region of total shadow is called the *umbra* and where this falls on the Earth the eclipse is total. The region of partial shadow is called the *penumbra*, and the places on the Earth covered by this shadow see a partial eclipse.

39

PROJECT 16 Moon watching

With your simple telescope you can make useful observations of many features of the Moon on a number of different days from New Moon to Full Moon. The 'age' of the Moon is the number of days that have passed since the Moon was in its 'New' phase. Actually we really cannot see the Moon when it is new because we are then looking at its dark side and it is too close to the Sun in the sky. This means that we see the Moon for the first time in a *lunar month* when it is a few days old. A lunar month is the time it takes the Moon to go from one Full Moon to the next (i.e. 28 days).

What you need

Your simple astronomical telescope (Project 14); Moon map (fig. 16.3); sketch pad and pencil.

What to do

It is always best to observe features that lie along the line dividing light from dark on the disc of the Moon. This line is called the *terminator* (see fig. 16.2).

Try, therefore, to observe the Moon when it is not quite full. The craters, mountains and 'seas' on the surface show up very well when the Sun's rays are catching them at an angle. On the map (fig. 16.3) is marked, very approximately, the position of the terminator for the ages of the Moon between one and thirteen days. The Moon's age for different days of the year is published in *The Night Sky* (published by *The Times*, see Appendix 4) or in the *Handbook of the British Astronomical Society*.

Once you have found the age of the Moon,

Fig. 16.1
The Full Moon

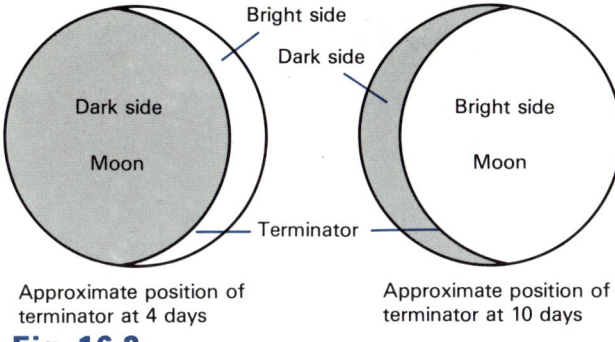

Approximate position of terminator at 4 days

Approximate position of terminator at 10 days

Fig. 16.2

look along the appropriate line on the lunar map and try to find some of the features on or close to this line. The surface of the Moon can be divided into two quite different regions:

(i) Lunar seas or maria. There is no water on the Moon so these seas are just flat low-lying areas of solidified lava covered with a thin layer of dust.

(ii) The uplands. These are characterised by many craters and mountains. The craters are saucer-like depressions of differing size with rugged edges and sometimes with a central peak. They were first named in 1651 by Riccioli (an Italian priest), who named them after famous scientists and philosophers. More recently discovered craters are named after professional and amateur astronomers.

Try to sketch what you actually see through your telescope. It is well worth practising this and will be useful in Project 21.

Remember: an astronomical telescope inverts the image so it is not suitable for terrestrial purposes – that is, it will give you upside-down images if you use it for looking at things on the surface of Earth. For astronomical purposes this does not matter much, but remember to invert your map of the Moon when using it with your astronomical telescope.

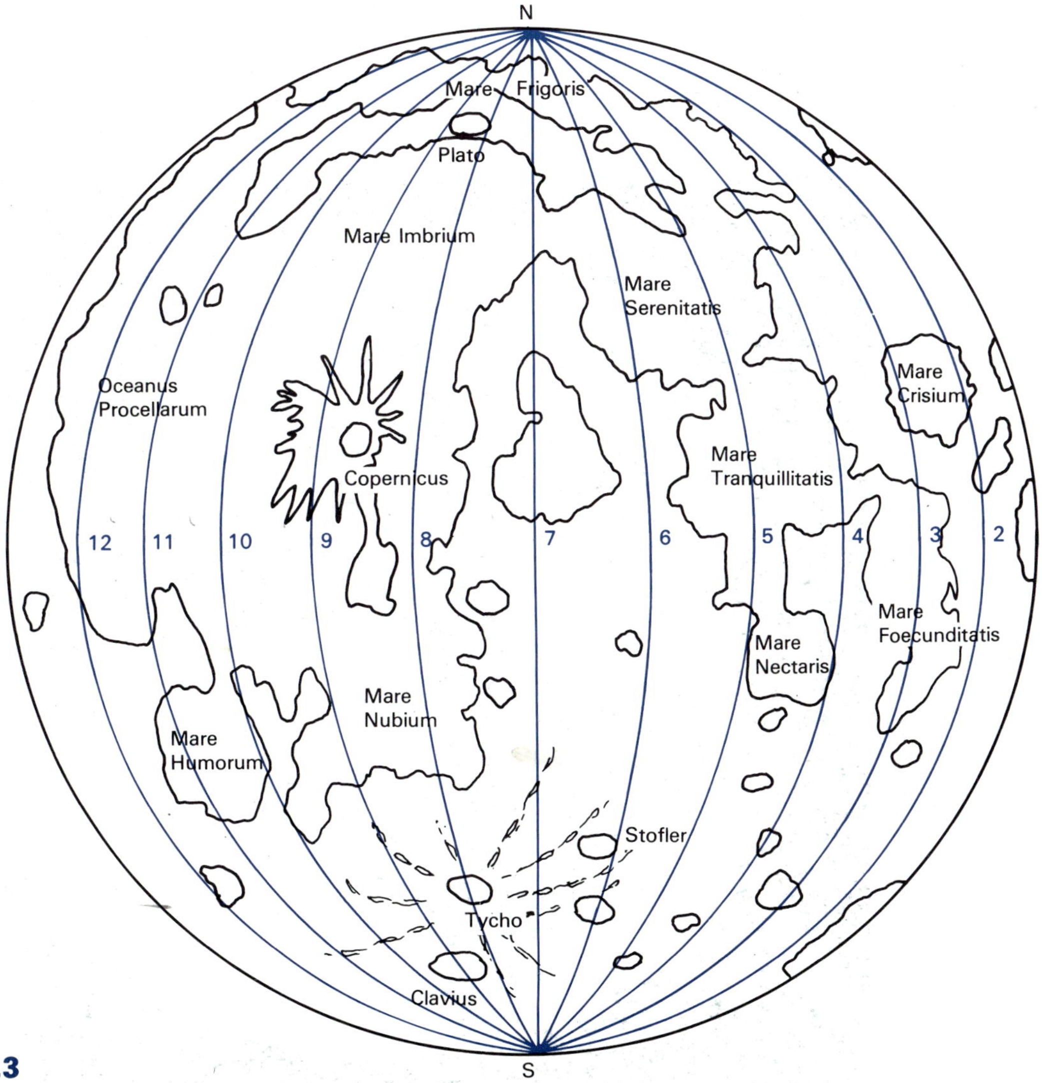

Fig. 16.3

PROJECT 17 Observing with a pair of binoculars

A great deal of useful observing can be done with a good pair of binoculars. In this project we discuss the principle, choice and use of binoculars for astronomical purposes.

The principle

A pair of *binoculars* is really two astronomical telescopes mounted next to each other. Each telescope contains two *prisms* which turn the normal upside-down image the right way up so that the right and left of the image you see is the same as right and left of the actual object (see fig. 17.1). However, the prisms also help to shorten the telescopes by bending the beam of light back upon itself, as shown in the diagram. The magnification is important, but so also is the amount of light that the objective lens can collect. This is why you usually find both these figures quoted on any pair of binoculars. For example, 8 × 30 tells us that the magnification is 8 times, and the diameter of the objective lens is 30 mm. The amount of light collected by the objective lens affects the brightness of the image, so for astronomical work people often use binoculars with 50 mm diameter.

Choosing a pair of binoculars

For most purposes a pair of binoculars marked 8 × 30 with first-class lenses is a good buy. It will reveal a great deal of interesting astronomical detail, and is a sensible instrument to start with. If you are going to use binoculars for a lot of Moon observations it will be worth getting a pair marked 10 × 50, or even 15 × 40. However, although the 10 × 50 has a greater magnification than the 8 × 30, it has a smaller field of view (i.e. sees a smaller part of the sky), and this can make it slightly more difficult to find the particular astronomical object you want to observe.

Much of the expense of binoculars comes from the fact that they use two very nearly identical systems of high quality lenses and prisms. They have to be nearly identical for the images of the two telescopes to blend successfully. If you cannot afford a pair of binoc-

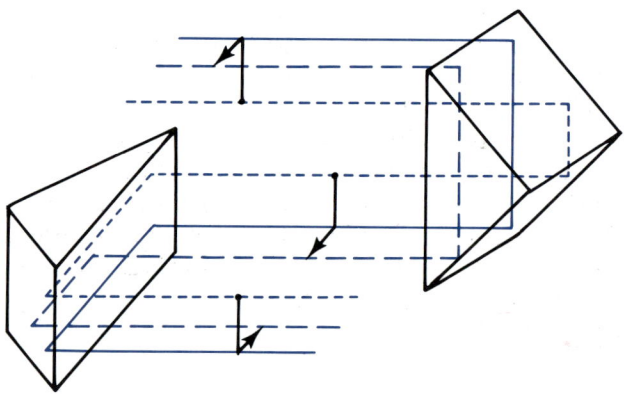

Fig. 17.1

ulars, you may be able to buy half of one, in other words a *monocular* (see Appendix 2 for suppliers). You might also be able to find one at a market or junk shop.

Using your binoculars

The main problem with using binoculars for astronomy is keeping them steady. Some observers mount their instruments on special adjustable mounts, but I prefer the suggestion by the well-known amateur astronomer, James Muirden: use a comfortable armchair for observing and just hold the binoculars in both hands, resting your elbows on the arms! It gives a steady, adjustable mount, and is comfortable if you want to observe for any length of time.

WARNING: Never look at the Sun through binoculars.

The Moon

With 8 × 30 binoculars you can see all the detail shown in the Moon map (Project 17), and you will probably see it with greater clarity than through your simple astronomical telescope. This is because, although the magnification is probably less than that of the telescope, the lenses of the binoculars are of better quality and produce images with less distortion and less colour around the edges. With practice you should be able to see features smaller than those shown in this Moon map. If you want to study the Moon in greater detail, 10 × 50, 12 × 40, or 15 × 40 types of binoculars will be more suitable. However, the prices of these instruments are such that you can make a telescope of greater flexibility (Project 19) for about the same cost.

Comets

In observing *comets*, binoculars are more useful than all but the most specially adapted astronomical telescopes, because they have a wider field of view. To find out when and where to look for particular comets, it is a good idea to join the Comet Section of the British Astronomical Society. Amateur astronomers using binoculars have made discoveries of new comets, so if you make this your particular field of study you could add your name to the list.

The Milky Way

In the Introduction it was explained that the Milky Way consists of a large number of stars, most so far away that they form a hazy band across the sky. You can see this hazy band clearly as a collection of stars through binoculars. A very interesting section to look at is the part which passes through the Summer Triangle (see Project 9) because it is particularly rich in the number of stars visible.

Star clusters, nebulae and galaxies

The Pleiades (or Seven Sisters) is a really beautiful star cluster which you can find in the constellation of Taurus the Bull (see Project 9). Binoculars will reveal many more stars than can be seen with the naked eye, and you will also be able to see the gas clouds surrounding the stars. Praesepe, or the Beehive Cluster, in the constellation of Cancer the Crab (Project 9) is another well worth looking at.

Nebulae are big clouds of gas in our own Milky Way. Many of these clouds glow because they have stars embedded in them. Two interesting nebulae to examine are the Orion Nebula, just below the three stars of Orion's belt; and the Crab Nebula near one of the horns of Taurus the Bull (note: the Crab Nebula is not connected with the constellation of Cancer the Crab). Use the star maps in Project 9 to help you identify the areas in which to look for these nebulae and the galaxies.

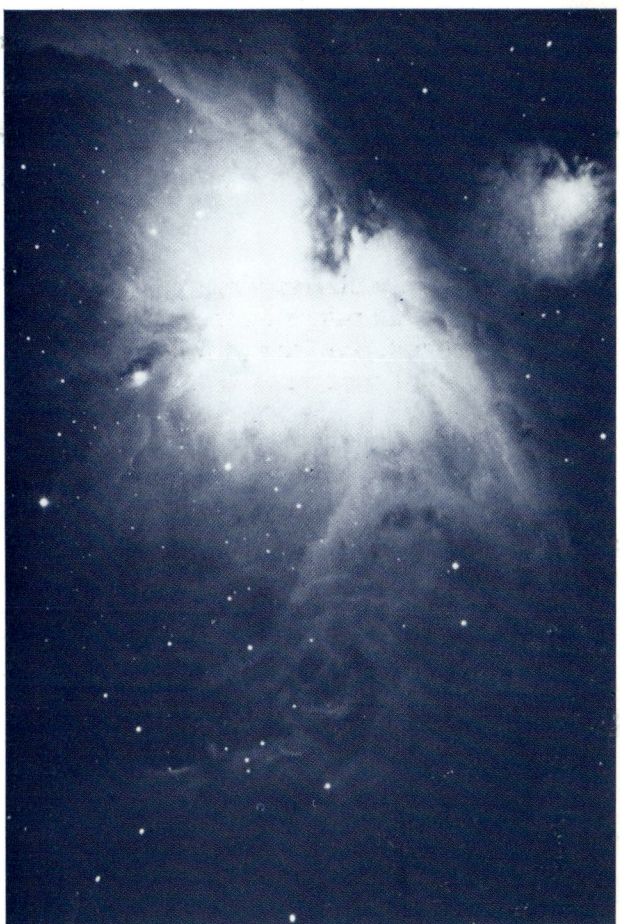

Fig. 17.2 The Orion nebula

The Andromeda Galaxy can be found by using the Great Square of Pegasus. It is really another Milky Way and consists of 150 000 000 000 stars. The Great Galaxy in Andromeda is the most distant object that can be seen with the naked eye, its approximate distance being 22 million million million kilometres away. The view of this galaxy through binoculars is better than through a telescope.

Planets

A view of any of the planets through a pair of binoculars is never very spectacular. Under good conditions it is possible to see Venus as a crescent with 8 × 30 binoculars. Mars can be seen as a very tiny disc but no features are visible. You might see four of Jupiter's satellites, but again you would be unlikely to see surface markings. Saturn can be seen as an elliptical source of light but you cannot separate the rings from the planet itself.

PROJECT 18 Concave mirrors

Most of us are familiar with curved mirrors, at fairgrounds, in cars or in our homes. Most really large telescopes use concave mirrors.

A curved mirror can, like a lens, form a real image (one which can be focussed on a screen, as explained in Section 13). As with converging lenses, the focal point of a concave mirror is the point at which rays from a parallel beam of light are brought to a focus. The focal length is the distance of this point from the mirror (see fig. 18.1). A ray along the axis will return along the axis after reflection at the mirror, while rays parallel to the axis will pass through the focal point after reflection.

If the distance between object and mirror is greater than twice the focal length (and this is always so in astronomy) then a real image is formed fairly close to the focal point (see fig. 18.2). This is a real, inverted image, smaller than the object itself. The difference between a concave mirror and a converging lens is that the real image is formed in front of the mirror but behind the lens.

There are advantages in using a mirror instead of a lens in an astronomical telescope. The objective needs to be large to collect as much light as possible from the object. However, lenses can of course only be supported along their edge and big lenses tend to sag under their own weight. Mirrors can be supported at the back, and therefore can be bigger than lenses. Moreover, with a mirror the light is only reflected from the silvered, concave surface and does not actually pass through the glass. This means that only one surface has to be ground and polished.

The next project describes how to make a good mirror telescope.

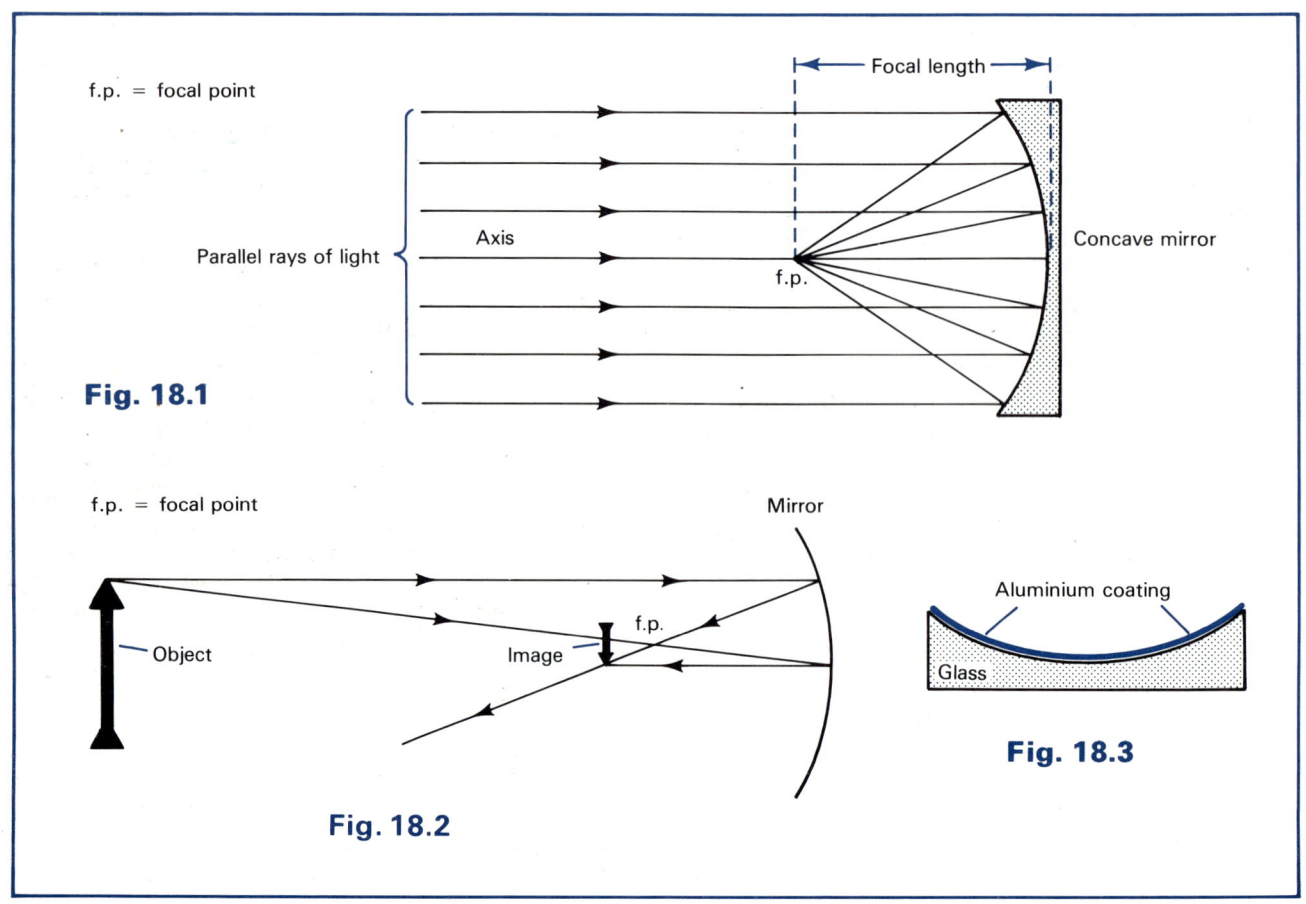

Fig. 18.1

Fig. 18.2

Fig. 18.3

PROJECT 19 Making a Dobsonian telescope

If you want to get a really good view of the planets and some of the other showpieces of the sky you need a good telescope. Apart from high magnification, it must also have good light-gathering power and this depends on the diameter of the objective lens. In the previous project we saw that, like a converging lens, a concave mirror can collect light and form an image. This means that the objective lens of an astronomical telescope can be replaced by a suitably mounted concave mirror. Isaac Newton invented a telescope using this method and most very large telescopes today are made this way. They have mirrors with very large diameters and therefore have good light-gathering power.

Good telescopes are very expensive to buy. Mirrors have only one surface to grind whereas a lens has two, so mirror telescopes are usually cheaper than lens telescopes of the same size. It is also easier to mount a mirror. In choosing a telescope you should make sure it has a firm mounting that does not vibrate when you touch the tube. Even good telescopes will give poor observations if the mounting is not firm.

An exciting alternative to buying a telescope is to make one yourself. You could start from scratch and grind your own mirror, but it takes a lot of patience and skill to make a satisfactory mirror so it is best to buy one ready-made. In this project we see how to make an extremely simple, but effective, version of a Newtonian telescope. This version was designed by John Dobson, one of the San Francisco Sidewalk Astronomers. You could make almost the whole telescope yourself, but I suggest you buy some of the parts, make the other parts out of plywood, and assemble the telescope yourself.

Fig. 19.1 shows the principle of the Newtonian telescope. Light from a distant object passes down the main tube and strikes the large concave mirror at the bottom of the tube. This mirror reflects a converging beam up the tube towards the much smaller flat mirror at 45° to the axis of the tube. This diagonal mirror reflects the converging beam out through a hole in the side of the tube. The enlarged image of the object is viewed through a focussing mount fitted with an eyepiece over this hole.

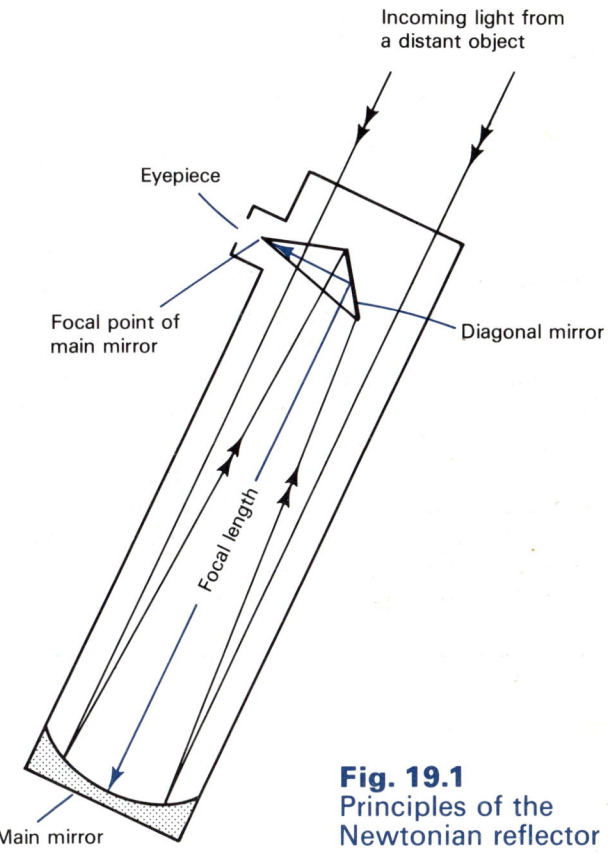

Fig. 19.1
Principles of the Newtonian reflector

Fig. 19.2 shows a completed Dobsonian telescope. The tube fits tightly into the rectangular plywood box which is fitted with two plastic side bearings. These side bearings rest in two Vs cut into the side boards of the cradle, which itself pivots about a screw through it and the ground board. The weight of the telescope and the cradle is borne by three Teflon (PTFE) pads nailed to the ground board. The ground board is fitted with three plywood feet. Attached to the box is another small telescope called the finder scope. This covers a larger area of sky than the main scope but at smaller magnification, and is used to find the object you wish to observe.

The list of parts needed to make the telescope is given below. The concave mirror, mirror cell, diagonal mirror, spider for supporting diagonal mirror, and the plastic tube should all be purchased together from the same supplier since it is essential that they fit together accurately. The focussing mount and eyepieces should also be bought together to ensure that the eyepieces fit the mount. Assembly instructions given below refer to parts obtained from Fuller-scopes, who operate a unit purchase plan enabling you to buy different parts at different times if you so wish. They will also assemble the main scope for you at no extra charge. Parts obtained from other suppliers may differ slightly from those described and you will have to adapt the instructions accordingly.

What you need

(See Appendix 2 for suppliers)

(a) Main telescope

1 concave mirror (aluminised) 22.2 cm (8.75 in.) diameter, focal length 129.5 cm
1 mirror cell to take 22.2 cm mirror
1 diagonal mirror to match concave mirror
1 spider and diagonal mirror support
1 plastic tube 127.5 cm long, 24 cm internal diameter, 24.6 cm external diameter
1 focussing mount
1 18 mm eyepiece
1 9 mm eyepiece

(b) The box – all wooden parts are made of 17 mm plywood

2 side boards   28 cm × 60 cm
1 top board   24.6 cm × 60 cm
1 bottom board   24.6 cm × 60 cm
1 wooden support disc 15.2 cm diameter
2 bearings, made of plastic drainage piping or similar, 7.5 cm long; internal diameter 15.2 cm; external diameter 16 cm.
24 × 1¼ in. No. 6 wood screws

(c) The cradle – all wooden parts are made of 17 mm plywood

1 bottom board   34 cm × 35.2 cm
2 side boards   34 cm × 45.2 cm
1 front board   35.5 cm × 38.6 cm
4 centring boards   8 cm × 43 cm
Sheet of Formica   35.7 cm × 38.6 cm
4 strips Teflon (PTFE) 0.15 cm × 1.7 cm × 10 cm
15 × 1¼ in. No. 6 wood screws
6 × 2 in. No. 8 wood screws
1 × 1½ in. No. 10 wood screw
Hardboard nails

(d) Ground board – all wooden parts are made of 17 mm plywood

Ground board   35.7 cm × 38.6 cm
3 feet   5 cm × 5 cm

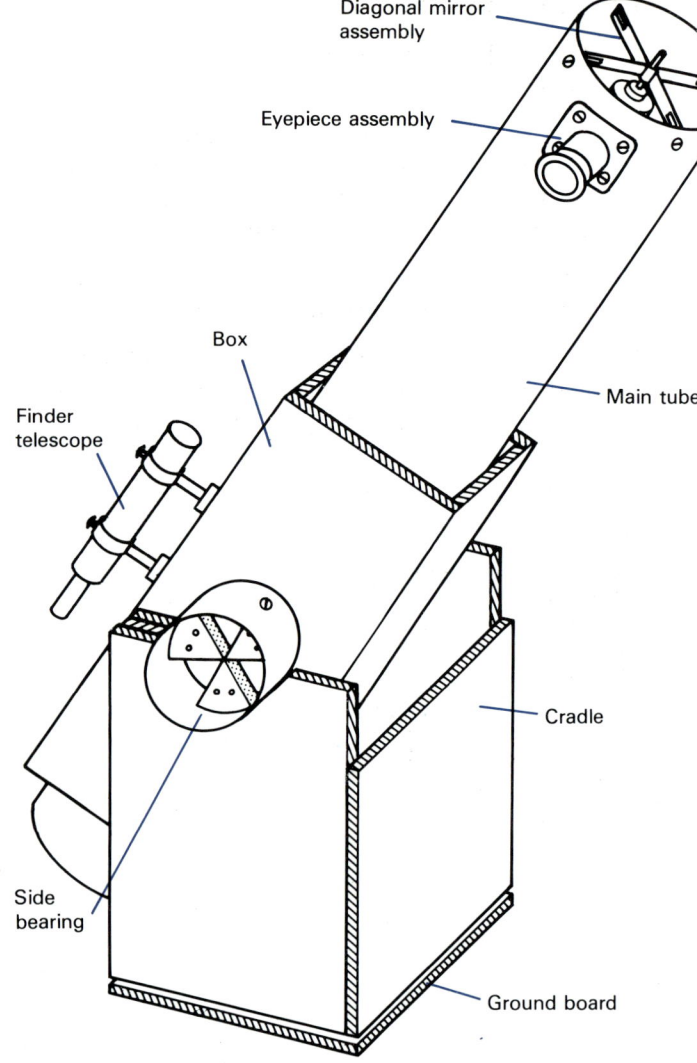

Fig. 19.2 The Dobsonian telescope

3 Teflon (PTFE) discs, 2 cm diameter, 0.15 cm thick
Hardboard nails
3 × 1 in. No. 6 wood screws

(e) Finder telescope

1 finder telescope 6 × 30
2 finder telescope supports

Assembling the telescope

Before assembling the main scope you may have to drill holes into the tube (if not done for you by suppliers) in positions shown and of sizes indicated in fig. 19.3. It may also be necessary to drill holes around the 3 cm diameter eyepiece hole depending on the position of the holes in eyepiece mount you are using.

Then proceed as follows:

1 Bolt spider in position on inside top end of main tube (fig. 19.4).

2 Fix diagonal mirror support into place in spider as shown in fig. 19.5 and wrap insulating tape around top of shaft to prevent mirror falling onto main mirror.

3 Bolt focussing mount to outside of main tube over 3 cm eyepiece hole (fig. 19.6).

4 Adjust height of diagonal mirror so that it is in centre of field of view of the focussing mount when you put your eye to eyepiece end (do this without eyepiece in mount) as shown in fig. 19.7.

5 Twist diagonal mirror about until you see whole of its surface through eyepiece end of mount.

6 Using the three adjusting screws of diagonal mirror holder, adjust mirror until the lower open end of main tube is in centre of field of view.

7 Fix concave mirror into position in its cell.

8 Screw mirror cell into position at lower end of main tube.

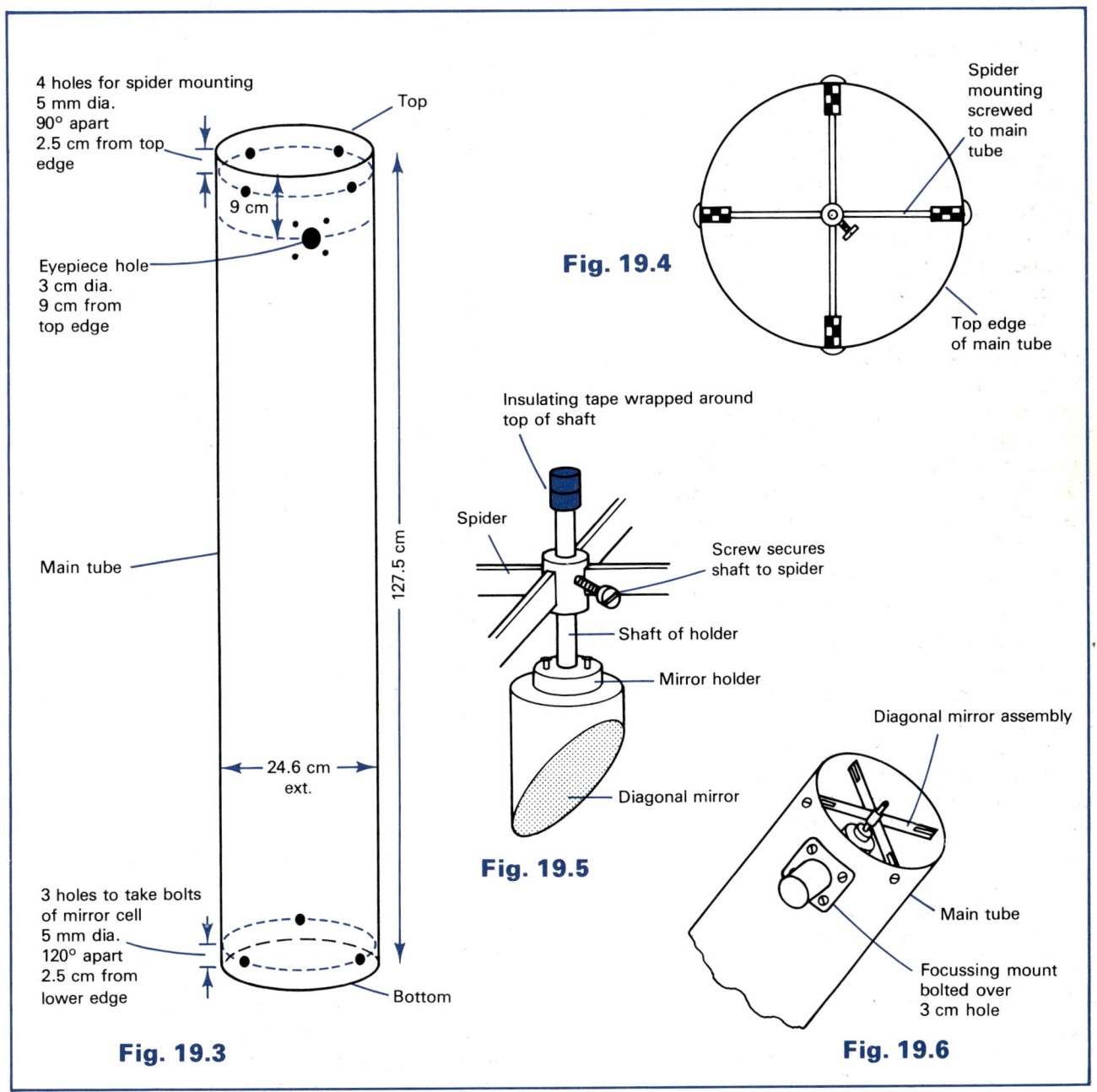

4 holes for spider mounting
5 mm dia.
90° apart
2.5 cm from top edge

Top

9 cm

Eyepiece hole
3 cm dia.
9 cm from top edge

Main tube

127.5 cm

24.6 cm ext.

3 holes to take bolts of mirror cell
5 mm dia.
120° apart
2.5 cm from lower edge

Bottom

Fig. 19.3

Spider mounting screwed to main tube

Fig. 19.4

Top edge of main tube

Insulating tape wrapped around top of shaft

Spider

Screw secures shaft to spider

Shaft of holder

Mirror holder

Diagonal mirror

Fig. 19.5

Diagonal mirror assembly

Main tube

Focussing mount bolted over 3 cm hole

Fig. 19.6

47

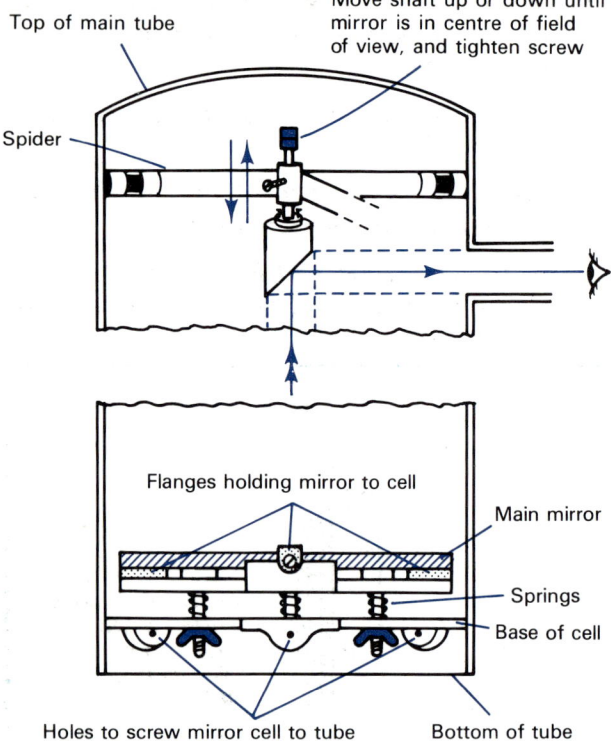

Top of main tube

Spider

Move shaft up or down until mirror is in centre of field of view, and tighten screw

Flanges holding mirror to cell

Main mirror

Springs

Base of cell

Holes to screw mirror cell to tube

Bottom of tube

Fig. 19.7

9 Using the three adjusting screws, adjust concave mirror so that it is looking directly out of tube. Upper end of tube will be in centre of field of view and you should be able to see your own eye (fig. 19.7).

Making the box

10 Mark diagonals on each side board of box to find exact centre, as shown in fig. 19.8.

11 Mark out a circle of radius exactly 7.6 cm around centre point on each board (fig. 19.8).

12 Saw plywood support disc into six equal segments as shown in fig. 19.9.

13 Arrange three segments to fit exactly in circle on each side board as shown in fig. 19.10, and screw into position.

14 Slip plastic bearing over segments on each board. Drill three No. 6 holes in each bearing through plastic tube, and screw bearing onto segments.

15 Drill holes into side boards and screw parts of box together as shown in fig. 19.11 (all screws should be countersunk).

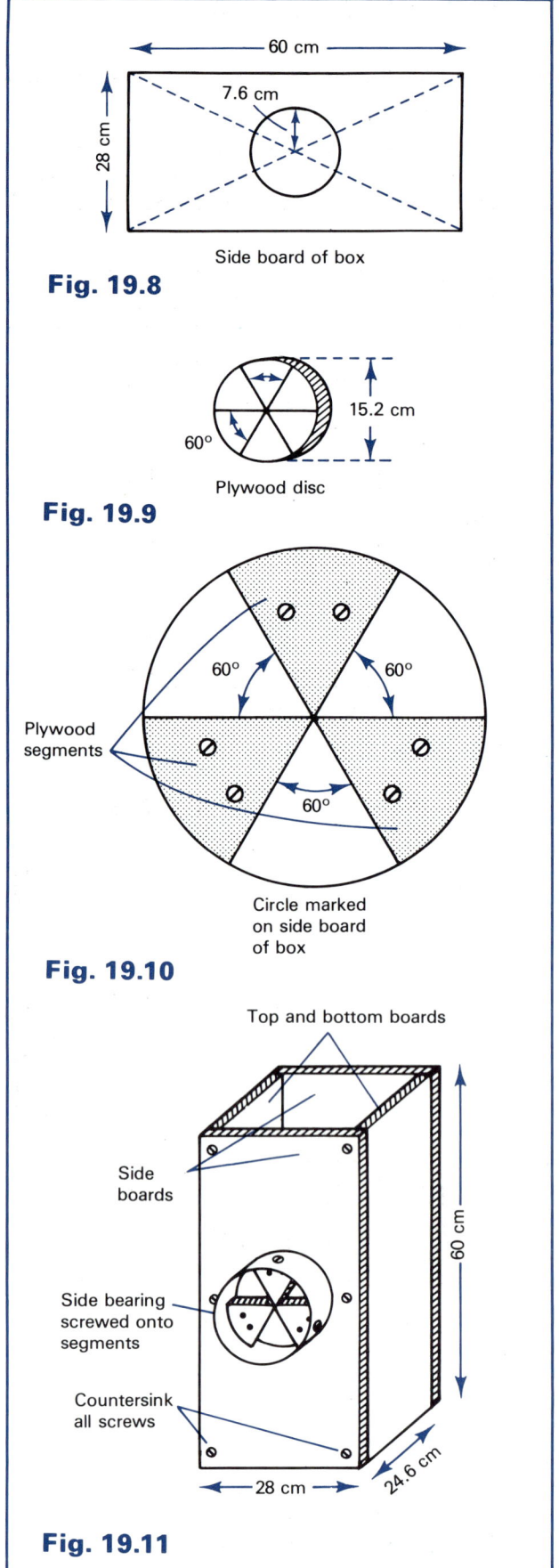

60 cm

28 cm

7.6 cm

Side board of box

Fig. 19.8

15.2 cm

60°

Plywood disc

Fig. 19.9

Plywood segments

60° 60°

60°

Circle marked on side board of box

Fig. 19.10

Top and bottom boards

Side boards

Side bearing screwed onto segments

Countersink all screws

60 cm

28 cm

24.6 cm

Fig. 19.11

Making the cradle

16 Cut a V-shape in top edge of each side board of cradle as shown in fig. 19.12.

17 Using countersunk screws, screw two centring boards along back edge of each side board, leaving 2 mm clear at bottom (fig. 19.13).

18 Using countersunk screws, screw side boards to bottom boards (fig. 19.14).

19 With countersunk screws, screw front board to bottom board and side boards (fig. 19.15).

20 Glue Formica sheet to bottom of cradle (fig. 19.16).

21 Drill No. 10 hole through centre of formica sheet and bottom board of cradle.

22 Nail two Teflon (PTFE) strips to inside edges of each V of side boards with hardboard nails.

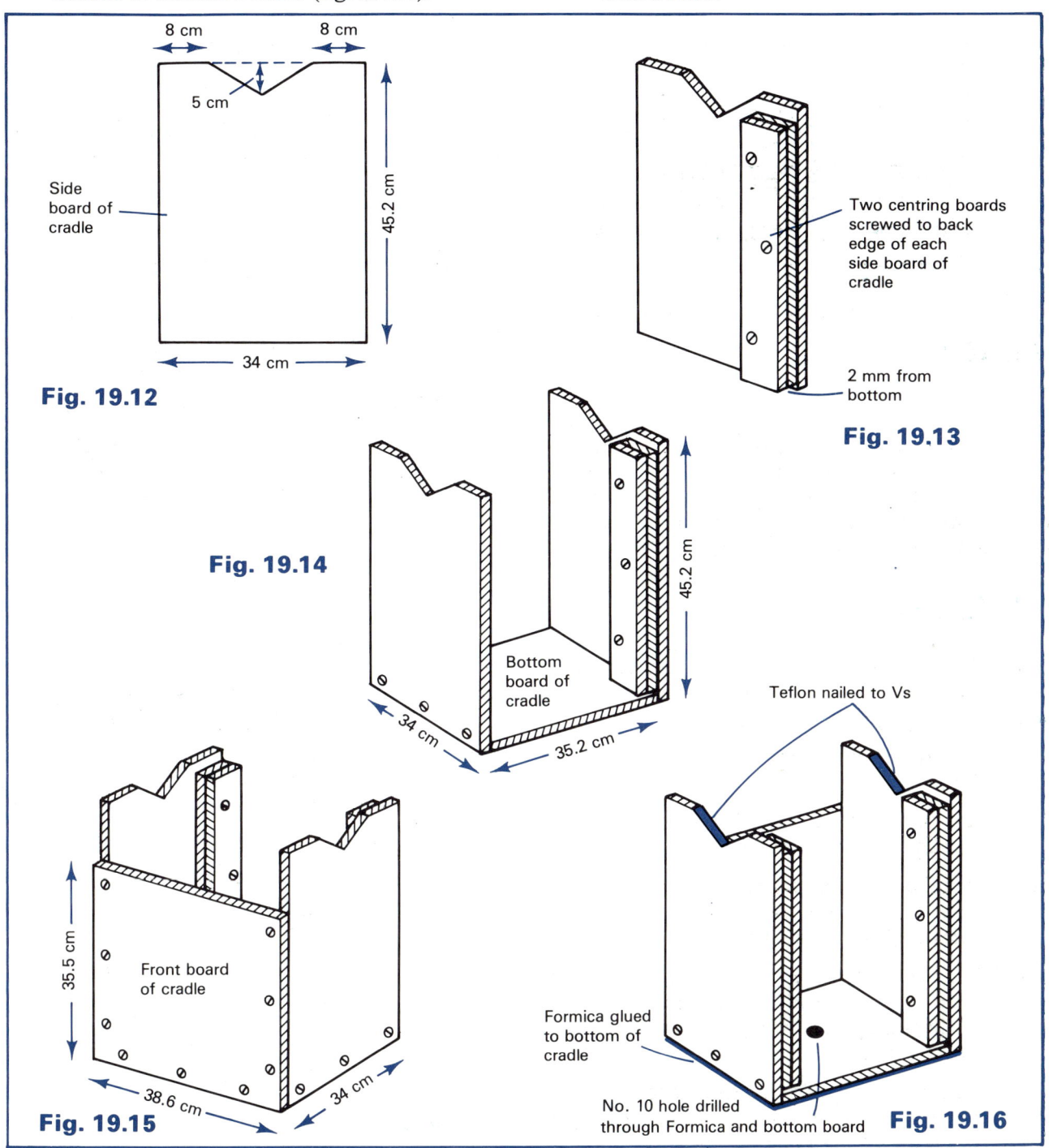

Fig. 19.12

Side board of cradle

8 cm — 8 cm
5 cm
45.2 cm
34 cm

Fig. 19.13

Two centring boards screwed to back edge of each side board of cradle

2 mm from bottom

Fig. 19.14

Bottom board of cradle

45.2 cm
34 cm
35.2 cm

Fig. 19.15

Front board of cradle

35.5 cm
38.6 cm
34 cm

Fig. 19.16

Teflon nailed to Vs

Formica glued to bottom of cradle

No. 10 hole drilled through Formica and bottom board

Making the ground board

23 Screw three legs to bottom of ground board using countersunk 1 in. No. 6 screw in positions shown in fig. 19.17.

24 Drill No. 6 hole into top of board as shown in fig. 19.18.

25 With hardboard nails, nail three Teflon (PTFE) pads to top of board as shown in fig. 19.18.

Assembling the whole Dobsonian telescope

26 Screw cradle to ground board with a 1½ in. No. 10 screw so that the cradle can swivel easily about the screw.

27 Loosen screws attaching side boards to top and bottom of box, so that you can slide main telescope tube easily into box.

28 Place box into cradle so that the bearings of box rest in Vs of cradle.

29 Adjust position of main tube in the box so that tube remains steady at any angle to which it is set. The telescope is now balanced.

30 Tighten screws of box to hold tube tightly within the box.

31 Attach supports of the finder scope to top of box so that finder scope will be half-way along top of box and to one side (see fig. 19.19).

32 Fix finder scope in position within its supports.

33 Fit the low power eyepiece (18 mm) into eyepiece holder.

34 Adjust finder scope so that it is looking at exactly the same part of the sky as the main scope. This is best done using the crescent Moon. With the lower power eyepiece find the Moon in the main scope. Move the main scope about until the cusp of a crescent Moon is in the centre of field of view (see fig. 19.20). Use the adjusting screws of the finder scope supports to adjust scope until the same cusp is in the centre of view of the finder scope. Repeat this a few times until you are certain that the cusp of the Moon is in the centre of view of both telescopes.

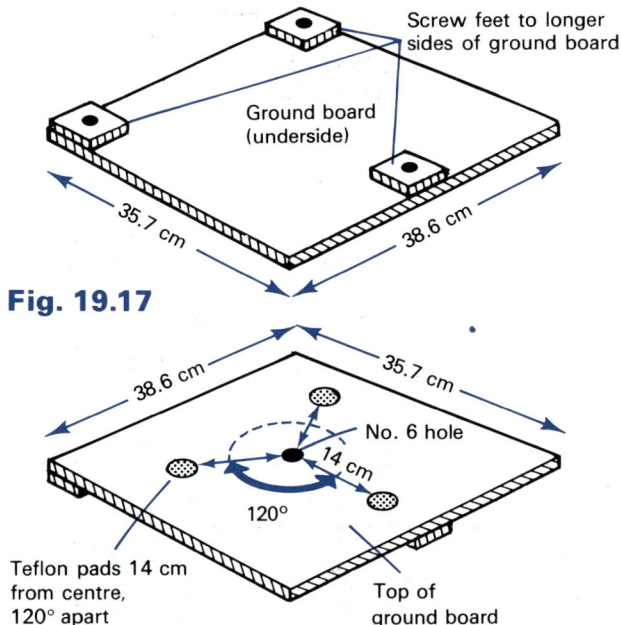

Fig. 19.17

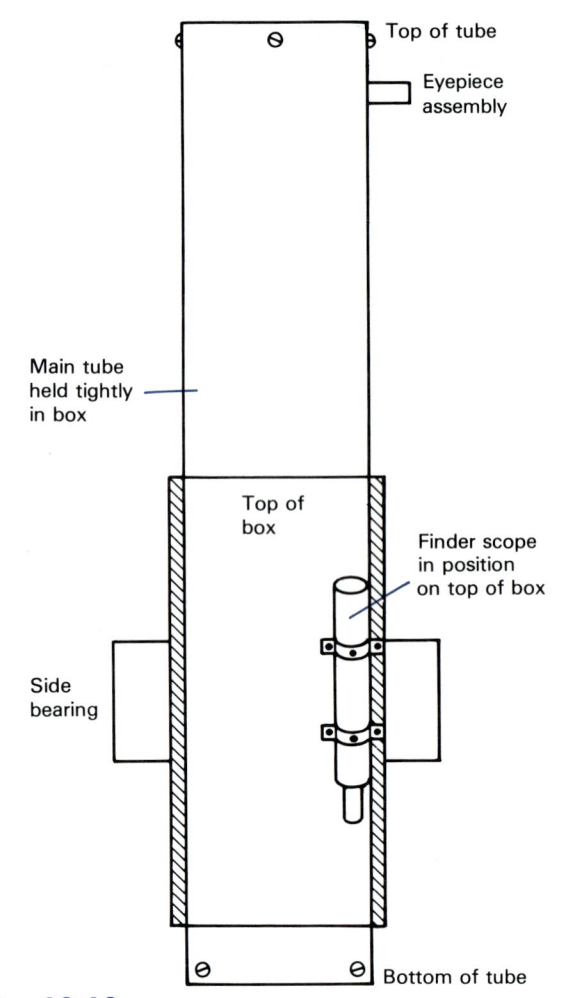

Fig. 19.18

Fig. 19.19

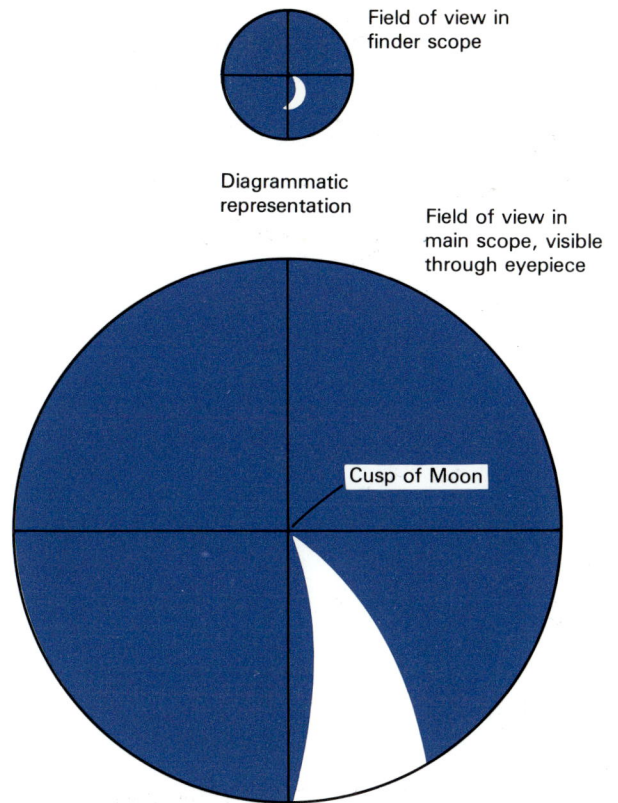

Field of view in
finder scope

Diagrammatic
representation

Field of view in
main scope, visible
through eyepiece

Cusp of Moon

Fig. 19.20 Diagrammatic representation

Your Dobsonian telescope is now ready for use. With the 18 mm eyepiece the magnification will be about 72 and with the 9 mm eyepiece it will be about 144.

Fig. 19.21 Dobsonian telescope made by the author

PROJECT 20 Using a Dobsonian telescope

With this telescope you can do some really interesting observations of the Moon, planets and stars. You will not always get the best results with the high power (9 mm) eyepiece. The air needs to be fairly calm when you use high magnification, so it is always best to start with a low magnification and build up to a higher magnification once you get used to the telescope and when conditions are calm and clear. If you start with high magnification without some experience, and when conditions are not good, you may be disappointed.

Observing the Moon

We have already discussed the basic observations of the Moon that can be carried out with a small telescope. With a bigger telescope you will be able to see much more detail on the surface of the Moon, so try to get hold of a detailed map or small atlas of the Moon (see Appendix 4). With this you will be able to identify many more features. However, a good habit to get into is actually to sketch what *you* see through the telescope. One way to do this is to make copies of the simple Moon map given in fig. 16.2 (Project 16). After you have found a fairly large feature through your telescope, fill in the details that you can see (but which are not shown) on the map, using a coloured pencil. Now use this rough sketch to draw an enlarged map of the area you were studying and on this fill in any other details which you can see. Once you have done this you can compare your map with a published map. If you really want to develop this ability

you should avoid looking at the published map until you have had a good try at sketching an area yourself. This will help you train yourself to sketch only what you actually see, rather than what you think you ought to see. *An accurate record of what is actually observed is the hallmark of a good astronomer.*

The planets

A general rule to adopt when sketching surface features of the planets is to use a pair of compasses to draw a circle representing the whole disc of the planet.

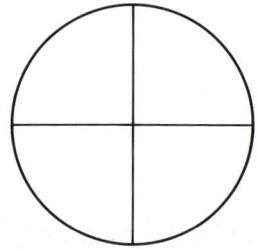

Fig. 20.1

You could if you wished divide the planet into four segments, as indicated in fig. 20.1. You can then fill in the features as you see them through the telescope. It will spoil your fun if you are told everything to look for, but a few remarks on each planet might be helpful.

Venus: As your telescope mirror will be 22.2 cm in diameter you should be quite able to see that Venus has phases just like our Moon. Sketch the position of the terminator (line dividing light from dark) within your circle represent-

Fig. 20.2
The phases of Venus

52

ing Venus. Do this as often as possible, both when Venus is visible in the morning and in the evening. Do you ever see the whole disc of Venus lit up?

Mars: All the planets are constantly changing their distances from the Earth and therefore they vary in size when seen through a telescope. This varying size is specially noticeable in the cases of Venus and Mars. However, you should be able to see Mars as a disc and with practice you should be able to see some of its larger surface features. You may even be able to see colour changes in some of the markings on the surface.

Jupiter: This planet is a reasonable size seen even through a 4 in. telescope, so with this telescope you should readily see that Jupiter is divided into a number of belts and zones. Sketch these on your circle representing Jupiter and study them for a few nights in a row. Can you detect any changes?

Saturn: Your telescope will readily show you the rings of Saturn. Can you see any markings, gaps or divisions on the rings, and can you see any surface features on the planet?

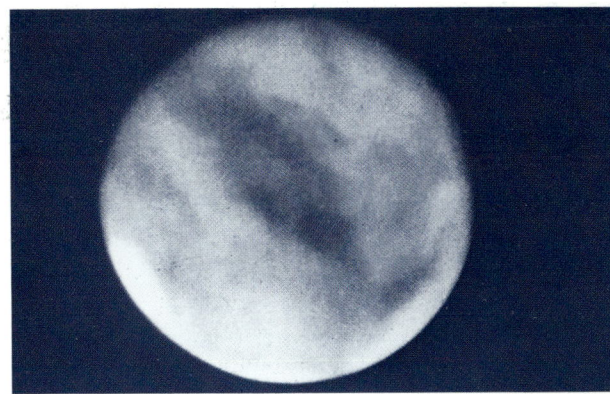

Fig. 20.3 Mars

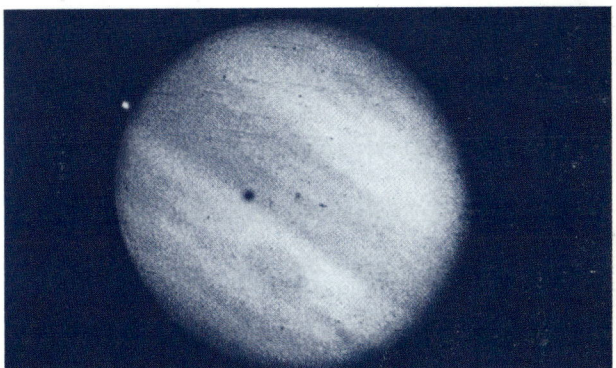

Fig. 20.4 Jupiter

Fig. 20.5 Saturn

The Outer Planets: The outer planets – Uranus, Neptune and Pluto – will all be visible through your telescope, and also in fact through your binoculars. However, you will need a good star atlas such as Norton's (see Appendix 4) and more information on the actual position of these planets on the dates on which you are observing. Information on planetary positions can be found in the *British Astronomical Association Handbook*.

PROJECT 21 Astronomical photography

If you have a camera that can take time exposures then with some additional equipment you can do simple astronomical photography (astrophotography). Some of these projects can be carried out by mounting your camera on a rigid tripod; others use a simple driven mount. For both types of astrophotography it is a good idea to fit a cable release to your camera to cut out camera shake.

Projects with a stationary camera

What you need

Camera, able to take time exposures; fast black-and-white film (e.g. Kodak Tri-X Pan); rigid tripod stand; cable release.

Star trails

On a clear moonless night, preferably far away from city lights, set up your camera on the tripod. Focus for infinity and have the aperture as wide as possible. Point the camera at a well-known constellation or an area rich in stars, and open the shutter for about 5 minutes. Close the shutter, wind the film on and repeat with openings of 10 minutes and then 15 minutes. Repeat with the camera pointing towards the North Star. When the film is developed you will see that the movement of the stars across the sky has given rise to star trails on your photographs, see fig. 21.1.

If you photographed a constellation the trails will be straight lines, and if the camera was correctly focussed for infinity the star trails should be sharp and crisp. If the lines are jagged it means that there was some vibration on the camera while you were filming. Photographs taken with the camera pointing towards the North Star should show star trails that curve in parts of a circle, because the circumpolar stars

Fig. 21.1 Comet Humason with star trails

Fig. 21.2 Circumpolar star trails

Table of meteor showers

Name of Shower	Dates at which seen	Constellation
Quadrantids	Jan. 1–6 (4)	Near the Herdsman
April Lyrids	Apr. 19–24 (22)	Lyra
η Aquarids	May 1–8 (5)	Aquarius
δ Aquarids	July 15–Aug. 15 (July 27–28)	Aquarius
Perseids	July 25–Aug. 18 (Aug. 12)	Perseus
Orionids	Oct. 16–26 (21)	Orion
Taurids	Oct. 20–Nov. 30 (Nov. 8)	Taurus
Leonids	Nov. 15–19 (17)	Leo
Geminids	Dec. 7–15 (14)	Gemini

(Figures in the brackets are dates of expected maxima of shower)

make circles round the pole of the sky, see fig. 21.2.

Meteors are often called 'shooting stars' although they have nothing to do with stars. Going round the Sun, in a similar way to the planets, are swarms of particles, small stones and some large boulders. These objects make up what we call a meteor swarm or shower. When our Earth meets such a shower, thousands of these particles enter our atmosphere where they are heated to very high temperatures by friction with the air. Most of the particles evaporate in the upper atmosphere, but they leave a trail of extremely hot gas behind them, called meteor trails. Meteor trails from a given swarm seem to radiate from a given point in the sky and so are usually named after the constellation in which they are seen. The table above lists the more important meteor showers seen at different times of the year.

Meteors can be well observed with the naked eye but can also be photographed with a stationary camera and appear as bright streaks of light cutting across the normal star trails. You need a great deal of patience to photograph a meteor trail. Set up the camera pointing in the general direction of the expected shower. Your photograph of star trails will have given you some idea of how long you need to keep the shutter open before it becomes 'fogged' by background light from the sky. When photographing meteor trails leave the shutter open for as long as possible without 'fogging'. If no meteor has occurred in this time, move on to the next frame on the film. Close the shutter immediately a meteor has crossed the field of view of camera, to ensure a bright image on the developed print, see fig. 21.3.

Fig. 21.3 Circumpolar star trails with meteor trail

Artificial satellites

If you are out on a clear night for any length of time, say 2–3 hours, you are almost bound to see an artifical satellite or two. However, if you want to photograph a satellite trail it is best to have some additional information on when and where to look for satellites on a particular night. You could get such information regularly by joining the Artificial Satellite Section of the British Astronomical Association (see Appendix 4). Once you have this information, set up the camera with lens wide open and point it in the general direction where you expect a given satellite to appear. Keep scanning the sky with your eyes and when the satellite appears, estimate its future path across the sky. Now adjust the camera to point towards the expected path.

Open the shutter and wait until the satellite disappears from view; then close the shutter. The result should be similar to that shown in fig. 21.4.

Fig. 21.4
Artificial satellite passing through the constellation of Orion

Making and using a simple drive for your camera

You know by now that as the Earth spins on its own axis the stars will seem to move about an axis which points to the pole of the sky. If you want to photograph a part of the sky without getting star trails or a blurred image you need to move the camera about the same axis and at the same rate. The device shown in fig. 21.5 enables you to do this. It is called a Scotch mount.

The camera is fixed to an adjustable arm which is attached to a bracket mounted on a hinged board. The axis of the hinge points to the north pole of the sky. This is achieved by attaching the hinged board to a bottom board which makes an angle, equal to your latitude, with the horizontal. This bottom board is screwed to an anchor block which points north. A drive screw

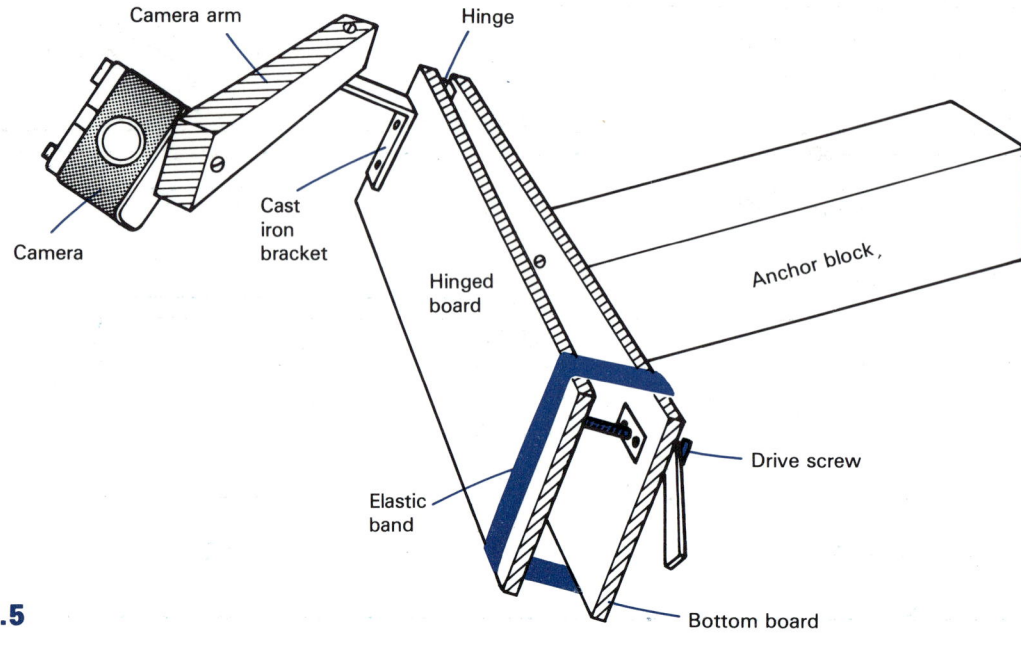

Fig. 21.5

passes through the bottom board and presses against a metal plate on the hinged board, and tension is maintained with a strong elastic band. When the drive screw is turned at one revolution per minute, the hinged board opens against the action of the elastic band at just the right speed to allow the camera to follow the motion of the stars. The camera can be pointed at different parts of the sky.

What you need

Hinged board, 9 mm plywood, 330 mm × 130 mm

Bottom board, 9 mm plywood, 330 mm × 130 mm

Anchor block, piece of wood 380 mm × 90 mm × 50 mm

Camera arm, piece of wood 170 mm × 35 mm × 25 mm

2 metal strips 1 mm thick, 40 mm × 15 mm

1 metal strip 1 mm thick, 50 mm × 15 mm

1 cast iron metal bracket 3 mm thick, 20 mm wide, arms 80 mm long

1 4 in. metal hinge

$2 \times \frac{1}{4}$ in. Whitworth bolt, $2\frac{1}{2}$ in. long

$1 \times \frac{1}{4}$ in. Whitworth bolt, 2 in. long

3 ordinary nuts and 2 wing nuts to go with $\frac{1}{4}$ in. Whitworth bolt

$2 \times \frac{3}{16}$ in. countersunk bolts, $\frac{5}{8}$ in. long

$2 \times \frac{3}{16}$ in. countersunk bolts, 1 in. long

4 nuts to go with $\frac{3}{16}$ in. bolts

$4 \times \frac{3}{8}$ in. No. 6 wood screws

$2 \times \frac{3}{4}$ in. No. 8 wood screws

1 strong elastic band

Drill with metal and wood bits

Camera

To make the drive

1 Saw anchor block so that angle θ is equal to your latitude, as shown in fig. 21.6.

2 Drill two No. 8 holes 30 mm from edges of bottom board, along centre line (see fig. 21.7).

3 Open out hinge and position on bottom board so that barrel of hinge is exactly flush with side of bottom board, as shown in fig. 21.8.

4 Keeping hinge in place, mark position of two screw holes (see fig. 21.8). Remove hinge and drill right through board to take $\frac{3}{16}$ in. diameter bolts. Attach hinge to bottom board with two nuts and bolts $\frac{5}{8}$ in long.

5 With hinge to left-hand edge of bottom board, mark a point on the board exactly 30 mm from top edge and exactly 291 mm from the axis of hinge (centre of barrel) as shown in fig. 21.9.

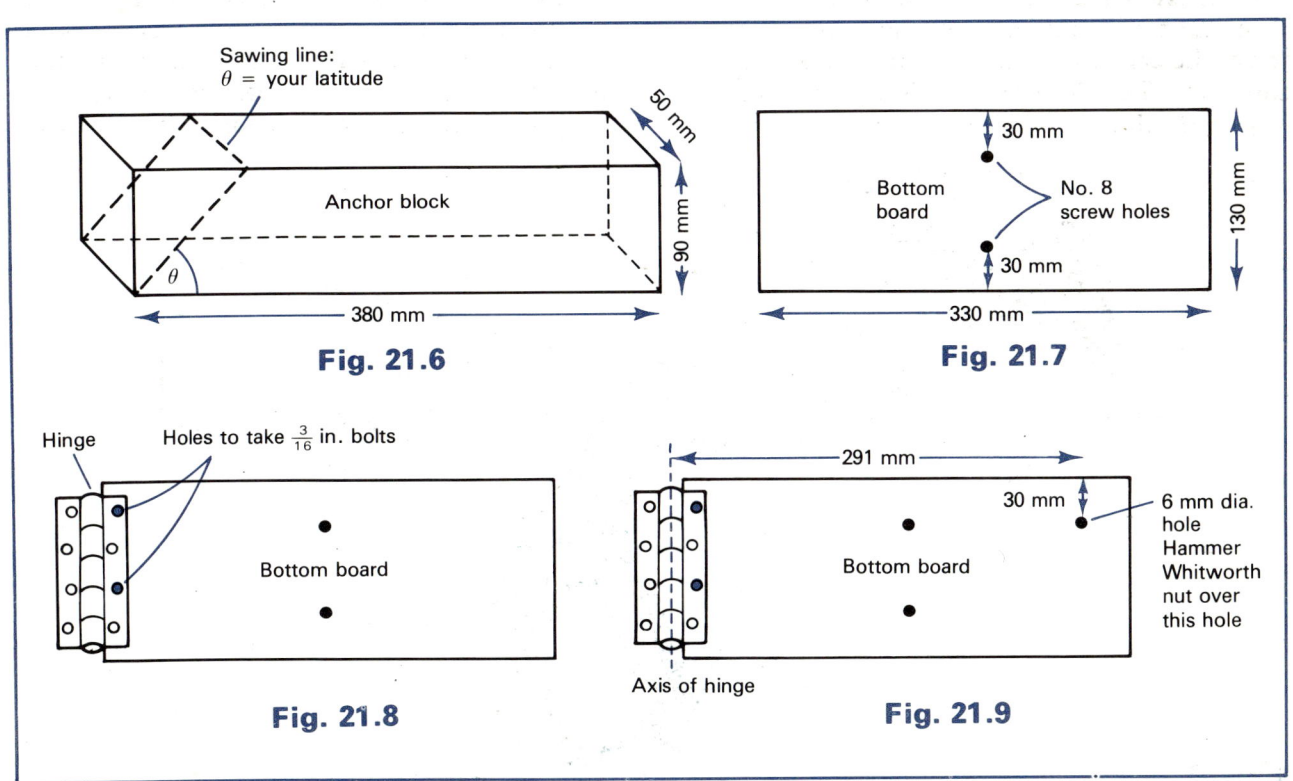

Fig. 21.6

Fig. 21.7

Fig. 21.8

Fig. 21.9

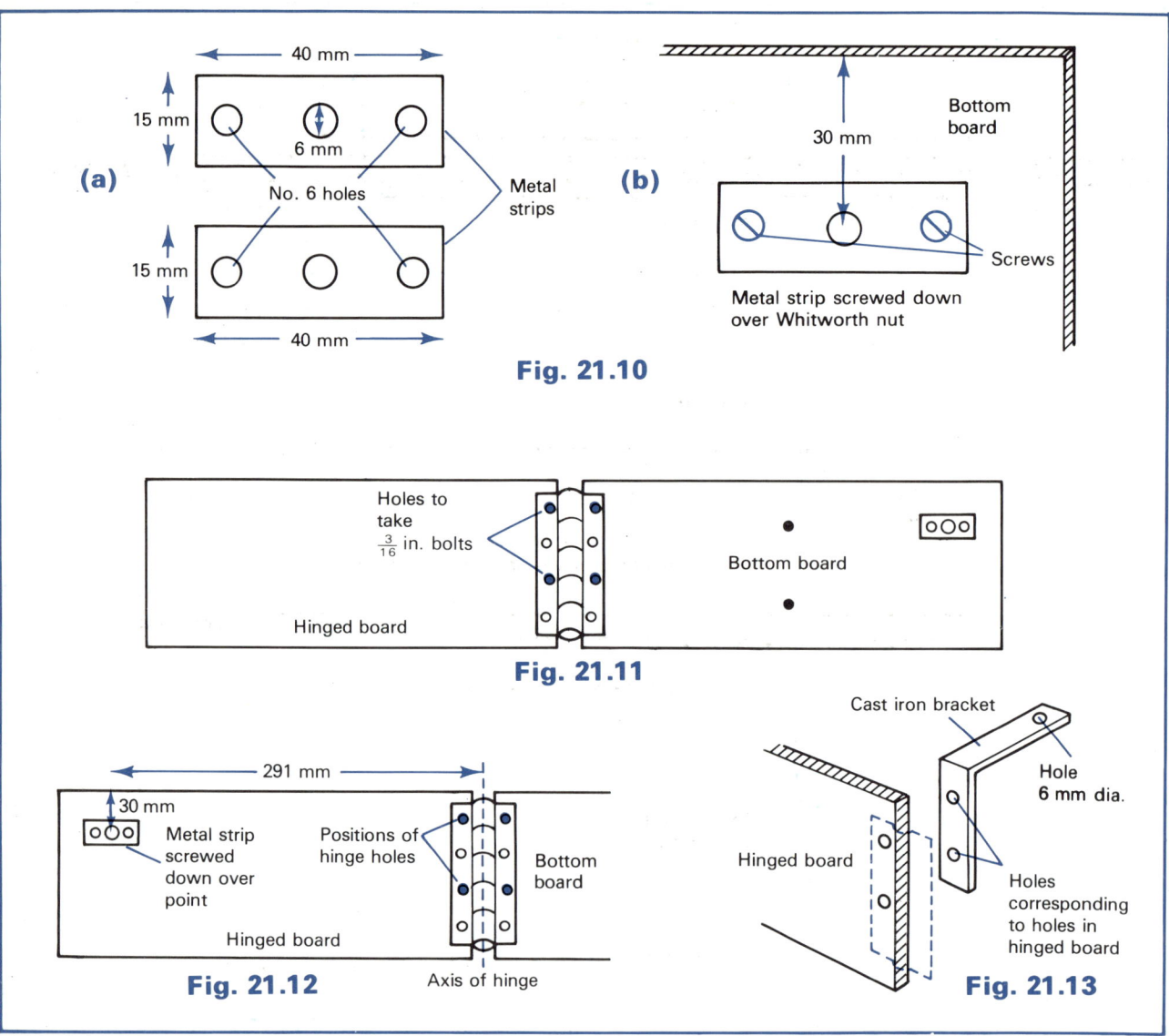

Fig. 21.10

Fig. 21.11

Fig. 21.12

Fig. 21.13

6 Drill hole at this point 6 mm diameter.

7 Over this hole hammer one $\frac{1}{4}$ in. Whitworth nut so that it lies flush with board.

8 In each of the 40 mm × 15 mm metal strips, drill two holes to take No. 6 screws, as shown in fig. 21.10a.

9 Drill a third hole in one of these strips exactly in the centre, 6 mm diameter.

10 Screw this strip immediately over the $\frac{1}{4}$ in. Whitworth nut on bottom board using $\frac{3}{8}$ in. No. 6 screws (fig. 21.10b).

11 Place hinged board under hinge so that edge of hinged board is exactly flush with side of hinge barrel opposite bottom board (see fig. 21.11).

12 Mark position of two holes in hinge (fig. 21.11). Remove board and drill holes right

through board to take $\frac{3}{16}$ in. bolts.

13 Keeping hinge holes to your right, mark a point on the hinged board exactly 30 mm from the top edge and exactly 291 mm from the axis of the hinge.

14 Over this point screw second 40 mm × 15 mm metal strip using $\frac{3}{8}$ in. No. 6 screws (see fig. 21.12).

15 Drill two holes in one arm of the cast iron bracket corresponding to the two hinge holes in hinged board (see fig. 21.13).

16 Drill hole in end of other arm of bracket 6 mm diameter (see fig. 21.13).

17 Pass two $\frac{3}{16}$ in. bolts, 1 in. long, through hinge, holes on hinged board, and cast iron bracket. Attach firmly with nuts (see fig. 21.14).

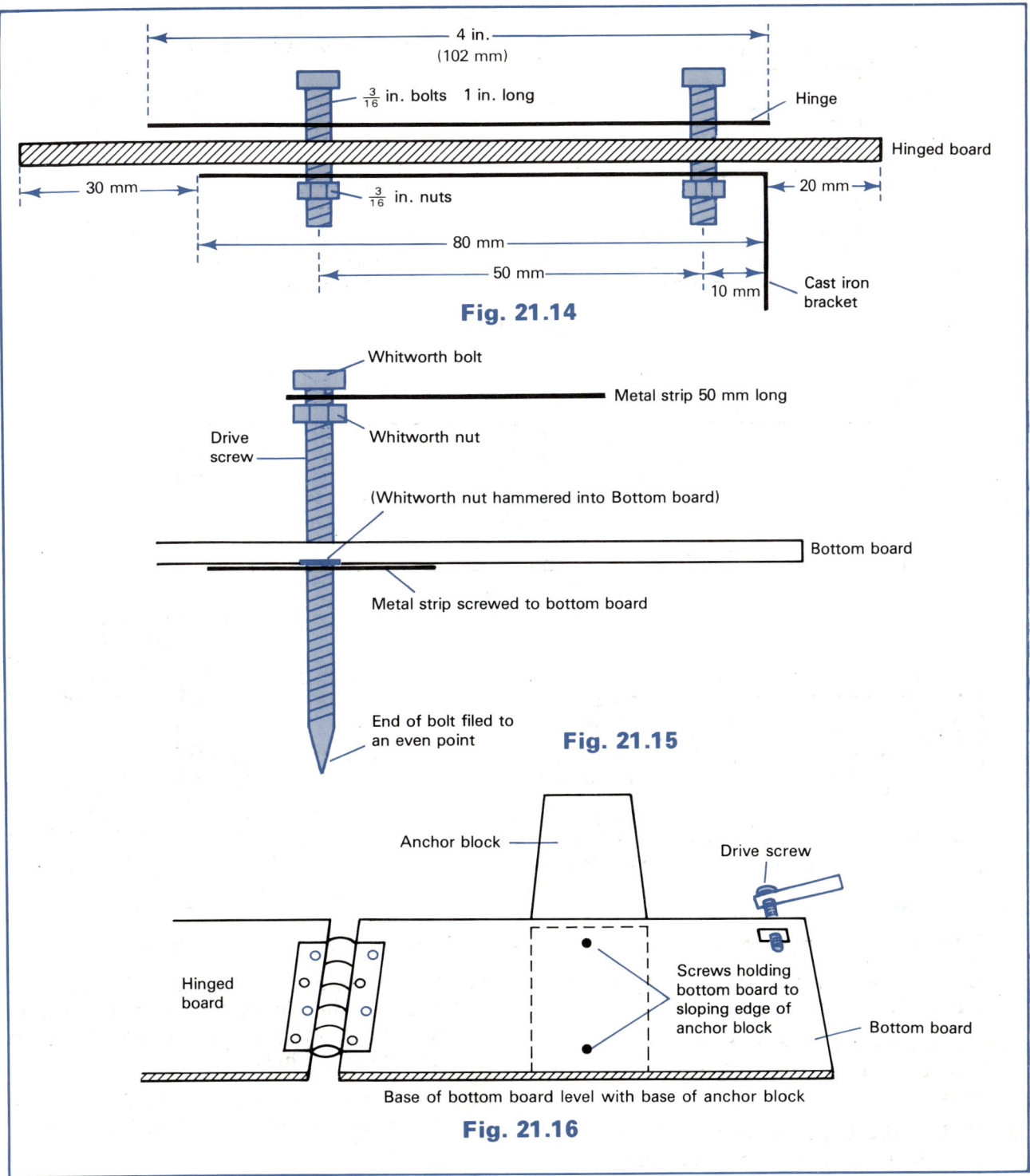

Fig. 21.14

Fig. 21.15

Fig. 21.16

18 Drill hole 6 mm diameter in one end of 50 mm × 15 mm metal strip.

19 Pass 2½ in. Whitworth bolt through this metal strip and hold firmly with nut. Screw bolt through nut in bottom board for about ¼ in. or so, as shown in fig. 21.15. This forms the drive screw of the mount.

20 Now file end of the Whitworth bolt to an even, rounded point as shown in fig. 21.15.

21 Screw bottom board to anchor block along sloping edge, so that base of bottom board is exactly at right angles to anchor block and level with base of anchor block as shown in fig. 21.16.

22 Drill hole 6 mm diameter right through height at one end of camera arm (fig. 21.17).

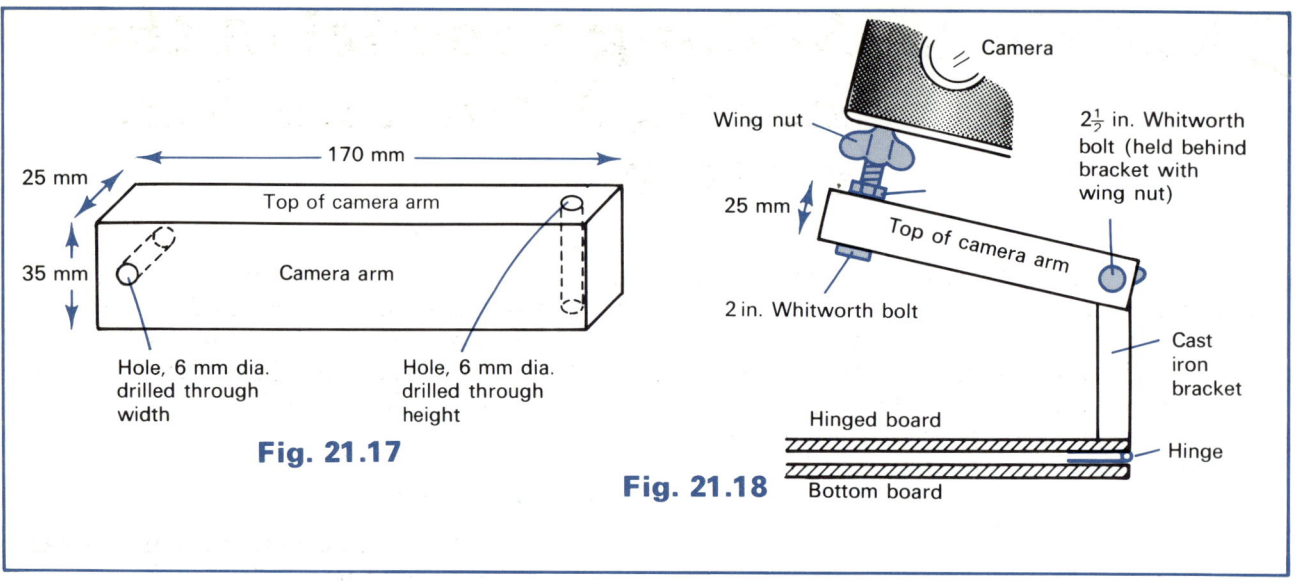

Fig. 21.17

Fig. 21.18

23 Drill another hole 6 mm diameter right through width at other end of camera arm (see fig. 21.17).

24 Pass 2 in. long Whitworth bolt through width of arm and secure with nut, as shown in fig. 21.18.

25 Pass $2\frac{1}{2}$ in long Whitworth bolt through height of camera arm and then through hole in end of cast iron bracket. Hold together with wing nut (see fig. 21.18).

26 Fold hinged board over bottom board so that rounded point of drive screw is in contact with metal strip on hinged board. Loop strong elastic band over both hinged board and bottom board to ensure contact between drive screw and metal strip on hinged board (see fig. 21.5).

27 Attach wing nut upside down to protruding end of 2 in. long bolt on camera arm and screw down so as to expose just enough bolt to screw into tripod socket on your camera. The maximum length for your tripod socket must not be exceeded or the bolt may penetrate the camera body and cause serious damage. Camera is kept in position by tightening this wing nut against the camera (see fig. 21.18).

The mount is now ready for use.

How to use the mount

Set up the mount with anchor block lined up in a north–south direction, sloping end pointing south. For stability, it is better to clamp the block to a bench or other support. The axis of the hinge will then point to the north pole of the sky. Using the winged nuts, adjust your camera to point to the desired part of the sky. Open the shutter. Using the metal strip as a crank, turn the drive screw at the rate of one revolution per minute. Use a torch covered with heavy red paper to follow the second hand of a watch. Close the shutter after the desired length of exposure – this should not exceed 10 minutes.

With this device you can photograph comets, planets as seen against the constellations, constellations themselves, nebulae like the one in Orion and the Andromeda Galaxy.

Fig. 21.19 Photograph of Orion constellation taken with Scotch mount

PROJECT 22 Making a model of the Earth, Moon and Sun system

Models of the Earth–Moon–Sun system can be seen in many museums and are often called *orreries*, because one of the earliest models was made for the Earl of Orrery. This project shows how to make a simplified model to demonstrate the causes of night and day, the seasons, eclipses of Sun and Moon, and phases of the Moon.

What you need

1 piece of wood 200 mm × 200 mm × 10 mm (called the base board)
1 piece of wood 300 mm × 20 mm × 4 mm (called the arm)
1 wooden rod 7 mm diameter, 147 mm long
1 wooden rod 7 mm diameter, 100 mm long
1 cotton reel 31 mm diameter, 33 mm long
3 cotton reels 22 mm diameter, 43 mm long
3 plastic washers, 35 mm diameter, 2 mm thick, hole 7 mm diameter
1 polystyrene sphere, 15 mm diameter
1 polystyrene sphere, 20 mm diameter
1 small globe (about 25 mm diameter)
1 small spherical mirror-like Christmas tree decoration, about 30 mm diameter
Flashlight battery, bulb and holder
300 mm PVC-covered copper wire
8 cm stiff wire – a paper clip will do
12 cm thinner wire, about 0.3 mm diameter
String, 3 elastic bands, insulating tape (cloth not plastic), drill, glue, Blu-Tack.

What to do

1 Drill hole 7 mm diameter in centre of base board, as shown in fig. 22.1.

2 Drill two holes 7 mm diameter each in wooden arm, one 30 mm from one end, the other 100 mm from other end (see fig. 22.1).

3 Drill hole 0.6 mm diameter, 15 mm deep, into top end of shorter wooden rod.

4 Glue longer wooden rod into hole in base board.

5 Slip thicker cotton reel over this rod, glue to base board and rod.

6 Slip plastic washer over rod, then slip wooden arm over rod through the hole 100 mm from one end, and slip another washer over rod (see fig. 22.2).

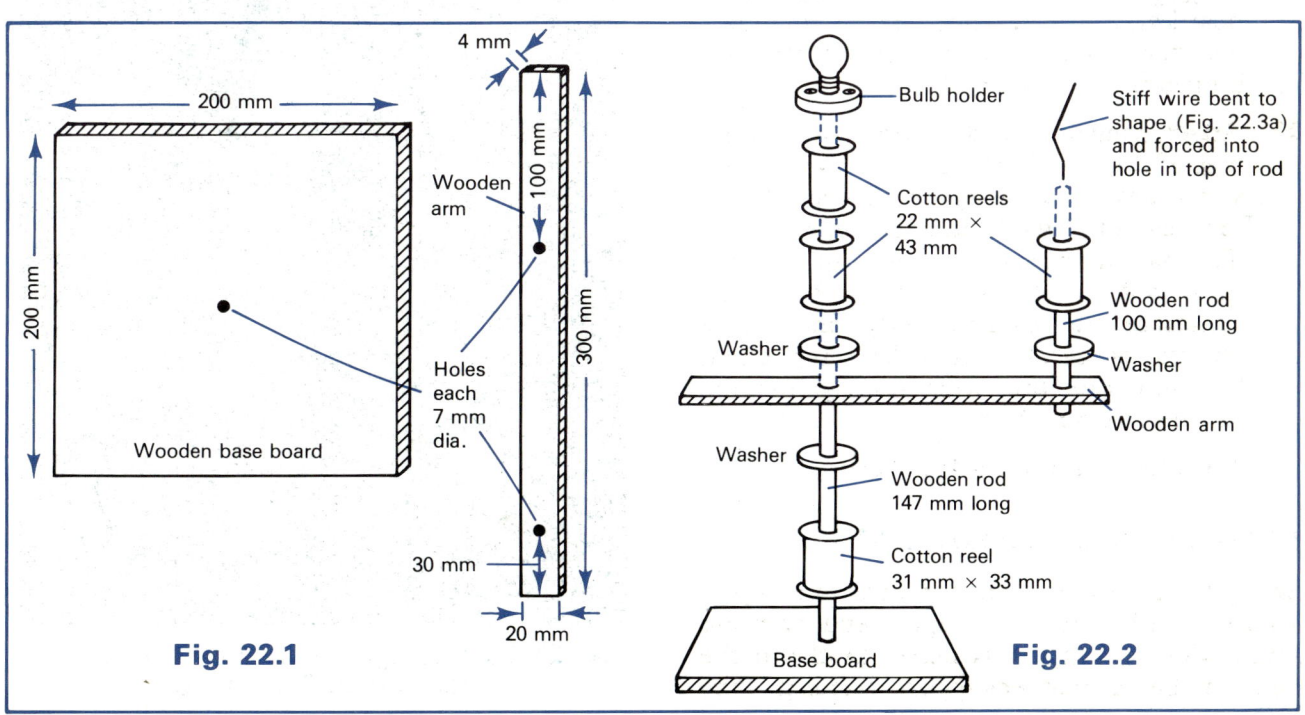

Fig. 22.1

Fig. 22.2

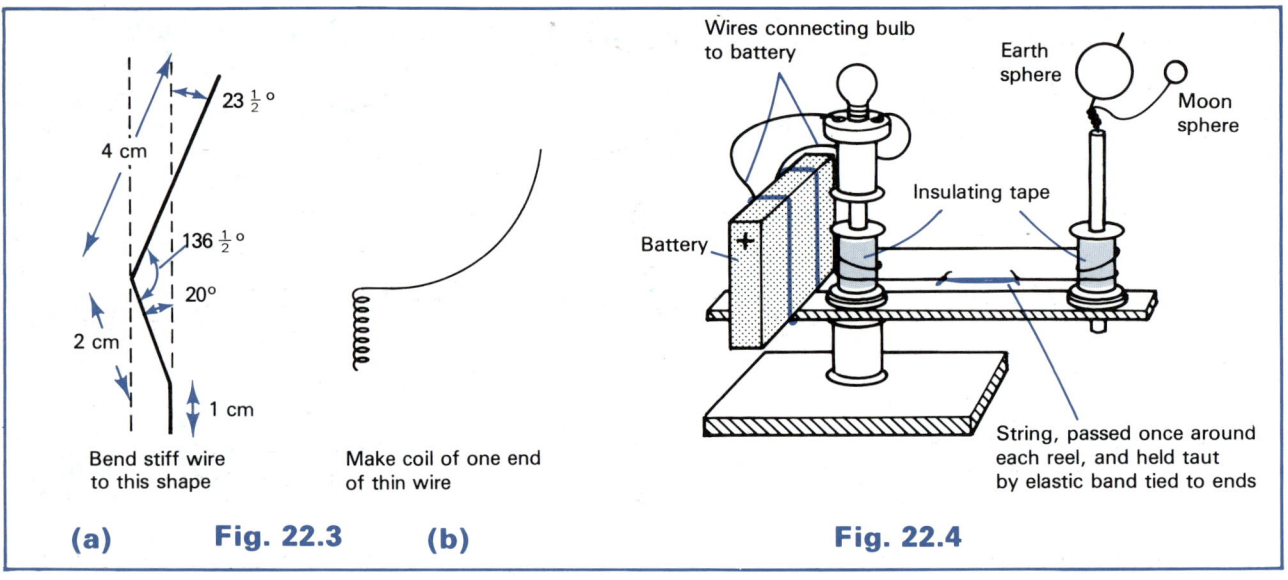

(a)   **Fig. 22.3**   **(b)**   **Fig. 22.4**

7   Slip one of thinner cotton reels over rod and down onto the washer and glue it to the rod so that it is held firm: the wooden arm should be able to rotate freely about rod (fig. 22.2).

8   Glue bulb holder to top of second thinner cotton reel.

9   Rub upper end of rod with sandpaper and then slip cotton reel and bulb holder over it. The reel should rotate freely about the rod, and the bulb holder should rest on top of rod.

10   Glue last cotton reel to shorter wooden rod so that 10 mm of rod protrudes from lower end of cotton reel.

11   Bend stiff wire or paper clip into shape as shown in fig. 22.3*a*, and then push 1 cm of lower end into hole in top of shorter rod. Wire should fit tightly into rod (see fig. 22.2).

12   Push lower end of this rod through a washer and then through hole in wooden arm (see fig. 22.2). The rod, with reel attached, should rotate freely. If it does not, remove rod and sandpaper it slightly.

13   Make a coil of one end of 0.3 mm wire and bend as shown in fig. 22.3*b*. Slip coiled end over stiff wire protruding from rod, and force other end into 15 mm diameter polystyrene sphere (which represents the Moon).

14   Earth is represented either by 25 mm globe, or by 20 mm polystyrene sphere, or by tree decoration, depending on which demonstration you are going to do. Each sphere

requires holes drilled through the poles so that the stiff wire can pass through them, as shown in fig. 22.4. Secure spheres on wires with Blu-Tack.

15   Wrap insulating tape around cotton reels resting on wooden arm (fig. 22.4).

16   Loop one turn of string around each of these cotton reels, and join ends of string with an elastic band to maintain tension in the string (fig. 22.4). Now, as you swing the arm, the string rotates the cotton reel with the Earth and Moon spheres above, thus keeping the axis of the Earth pointing in the same direction with respect to the distant stars.

17   Connect battery to bulb holder and secure to wooden arm with elastic bands (fig. 22.4).

Using the model

For the first two demonstrations, use the 25 mm globe for the Earth and bend the Moon sphere down out of the way.

Day and Night: On the Earth globe you will notice that lines of longitude go from North Pole to South Pole. These lines are 15° apart and each 15° turn is called a time zone. Turn the Earth globe about its own axis until Greenwich Meridian is opposite the bulb (which represents the Sun). Along the Greenwich Meridian it will now be noon. Along the 180° line of longitude round the other side (called the *International Date Line*) it will be midnight. As you rotate the globe so each given point along the Greenwich Meridian will in turn cross a line dividing the light from the bulb from shadow (day from night). Any point on the Earth, as it

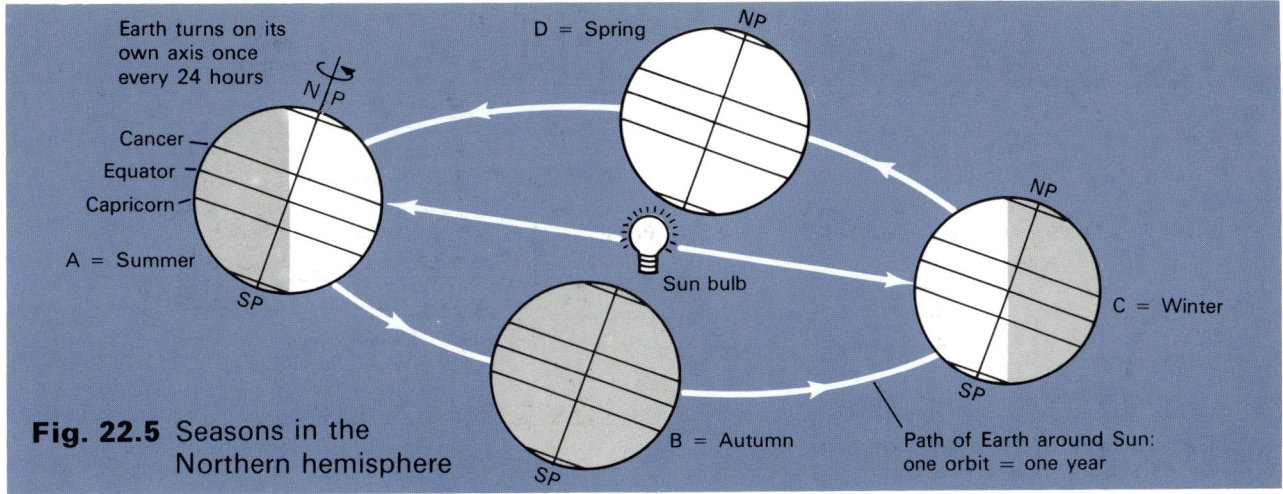

Fig. 22.5 Seasons in the Northern hemisphere

leaves the light, enters dusk and then moves into dark region, and as it emerges around the other side it goes through dawn and then comes into daylight again.

The seasons: The positions shown as A, B, C and D on fig. 22.5 represent midsummer,

dividing light from dark passes through the poles, the Sun is directly overhead at the Equator, and all over the world there will be equal hours of day and night. These positions are called the *equinoxes* (which means equal day and night).

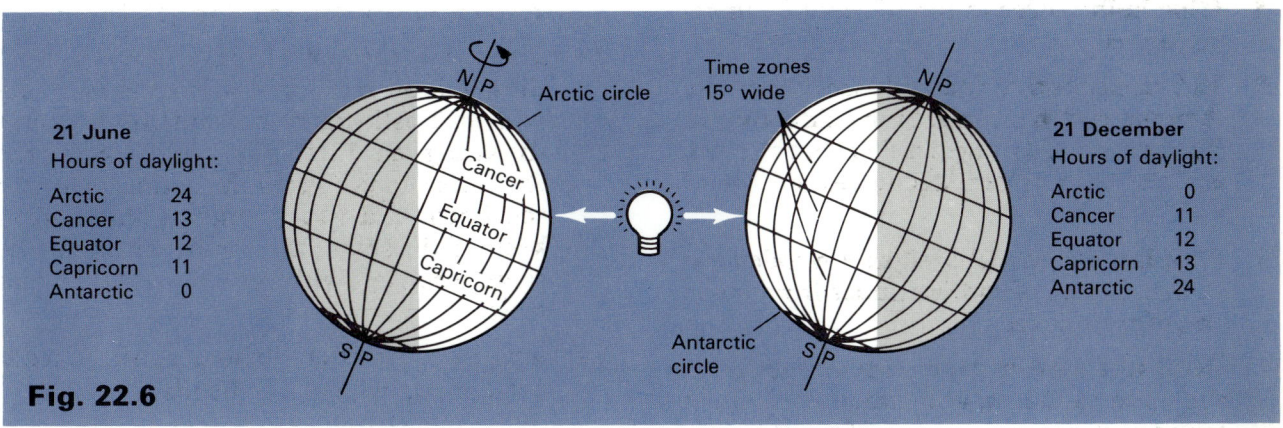

Fig. 22.6

autumn equinox, midwinter and spring equinox. In position A, you will notice that the Tropic of Cancer is directly opposite bulb, so on this line of latitude on the Earth the Sun will be directly overhead at noon. As you turn the globe you notice that the region north of the Arctic Circle remains in light all the time, so here they will be having 24 hours of daylight on this particular day, which we call Midsummer's Day. You can also find length of day and night at any latitude by counting the number of zones in the light and dark regions respectively. You will find that day length increases as you go from the South Pole (where it is zero on this day) to the North Pole. Fig. 22.6 makes this clear. Position C is just the reverse of A, and of course it is now dark for 24 hours at the North Pole and light for 24 hours at the South Pole. In positions B and D the line

Phases of the Moon: Use the Christmas tree decoration to represent the Earth. Adjust the model so that the Moon is behind the Earth as seen from the Sun, but higher (or lower) than the imaginary line joining the Sun to the Earth, as shown in fig. 22.7*a*. This is the Full Moon position, as can be seen from fig. 22.7*b* (C). As seen from the Earth, the whole face of the Moon will be lit up and its dark side is facing away from the Earth. Look into the mirror surface of the Earth sphere, and you will see reflected the view of the Moon that is seen from the Earth, but reversed. The positions A, B and D shown in fig. 22.7*b* represent the positions of the New Moon, First Quarter and Third Quarter. Once again, you can get the Earth-bound view (reversed) of these phases by looking into the mirror surface of the sphere.

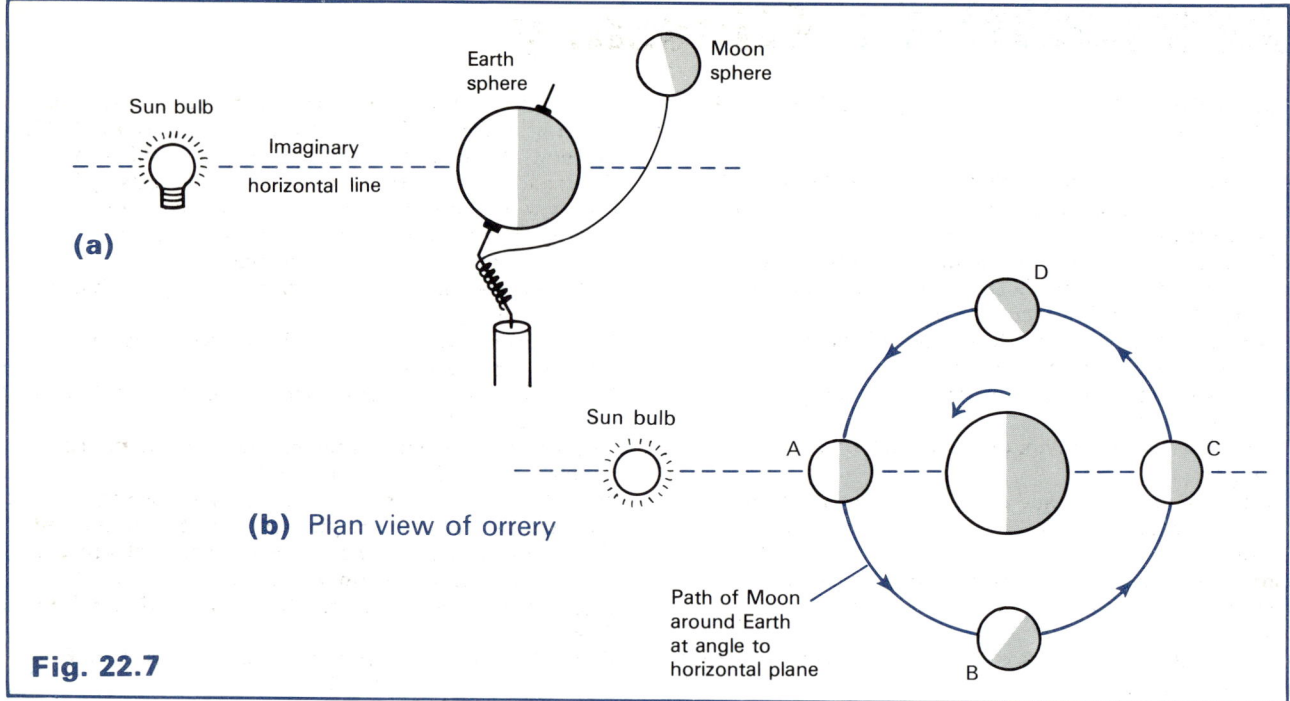

(a)

(b) Plan view of orrery

Path of Moon around Earth at angle to horizontal plane

Fig. 22.7

Eclipses: Paint the bulb white for this demonstration, and use the polystyrene sphere to represent the Earth. Adjust model until the Moon is between the Sun and the Earth and the shadow of the Moon falls on the Earth sphere, as shown in fig. 22.8a. You will notice that there are two regions to this shadow. The region of total shadow is very dark, and this area is called the umbra (as was explained in Project 15): at this point on the Earth people would see a total eclipse of the Sun. The region outside this shadow is less dark and is called the penumbra: in this region people on the Earth would see a partial eclipse of the Sun. An eclipse of the Moon occurs when the Moon is completely in the shadow of the Earth. Adjust model so that the Sun, Earth and Moon are in a straight line (fig. 22.8b). The Moon will then be in the shadow of the Earth. You may think we should not be able to see the Moon at all during a total eclipse, but some of the red light from the Sun is bent around the Earth by our atmosphere and so the Moon does have a reddish colour during a total eclipse. Notice also that this is not the same as New Moon when for a while we also do not see the Moon.

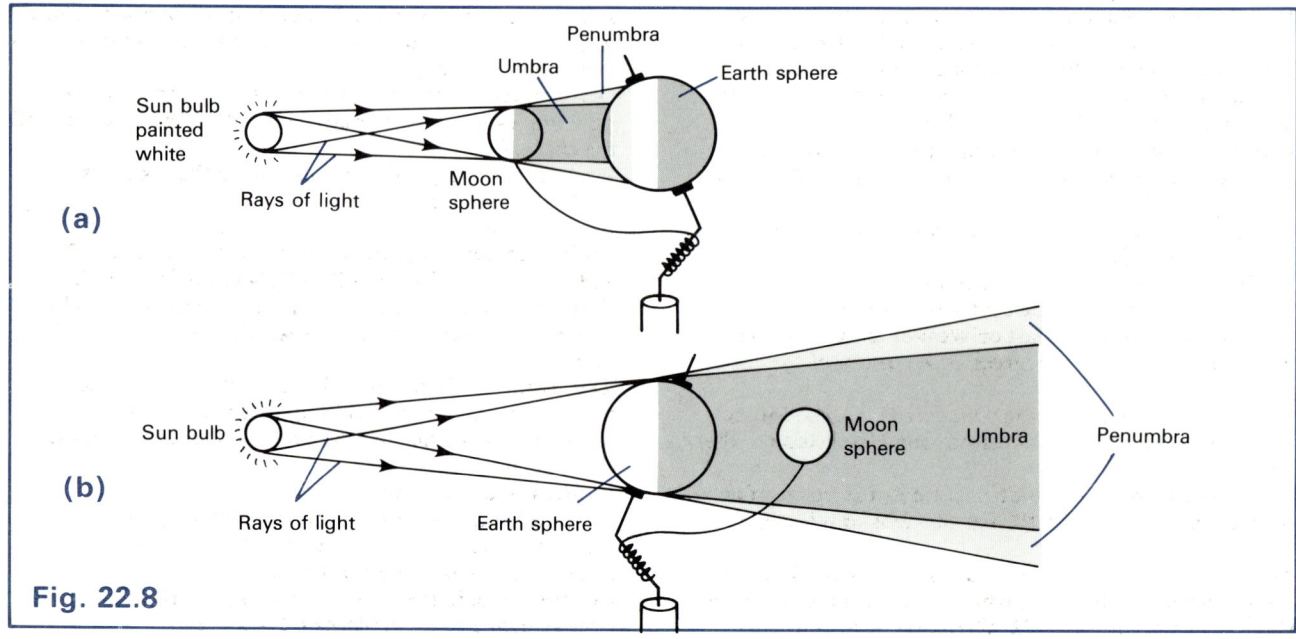

Fig. 22.8

APPENDIX I Glossary

The numbers in brackets refer to the project in which the term is first mentioned.

Annular – ring-shaped or ring-like. **Annular eclipse –** one in which the Moon does not eclipse the whole of the Sun, so the Sun is seen as a ring. (15)

Alt-azimuth – Instrument for measuring the height of a heavenly body above the horizon and the angle it makes with the North or South points. (6)

Altitude – The height of a heavenly body above the horizon, measured in degrees. (6)

Azimuth – The angle a body makes with the north or south points. (6)

Asteroid – One of the minor planets orbiting the Sun. (Intro.)

Circumpolar – Stars and constellations which circle round the pole of the sky, but never set below the horizon. (6)

Comet – A gaseous body orbiting the Sun. A comet only becomes visible to the naked eye when it is close to the Sun. (Intro.)

Constellation – A group of stars linked together to form a shape in the sky. (7)

Eclipse – The light from a distant object is said to be eclipsed when a nearer object comes between the Earth and the first object. A solar eclipse occurs when the Moon comes between the Earth and the Sun. A lunar eclipse occurs when the shadow of the Earth falls on the Moon. (15)

Ellipse – Oval-shaped figure. Almost all the bodies that orbit the Sun have elliptical orbits. (Intro.)

Eyepiece – The lens system at the end of a telescope through which the eye looks. (13)

Equator – A circle of latitude, midway between the North and South Poles, dividing the surface of the Earth in half. (2)

Equinoxes – (Spring E. and Autumn E.) Position of Earth in relation to Sun on the two days of year when Sun is directly overhead at Equator. On these days we have equal hours of day and night all over the world.

Fixed stars – Stars which do not change their positions with respect to each other as seen from the Earth over very long periods of time. This includes all the stars. Powerful telescopes have, however, shown us that all the stars have some slight motion. (Intro.)

Galaxy – A very large collection of stars, containing thousands of millions of stars. Our own Milky Way is but one example. (Intro.)

Gnomon – Part of a sundial that casts a shadow on the face of the dial. (4)

Latitude – Distance North or South of the Equator, measured in degrees at the centre of the Earth. (2)

Longitude – Distance East or West of the Greenwich Meridian, measured in degrees at the centre of the Earth. (2)

Lunar – Adjective meaning connected with the Moon. (16) **Lunar Month** – Period from one New Moon to the next. (16)

Magnification – The number of times the image of an object is made bigger by the use of a lens or telescope. (13)

Meridian – Your local meridian is the North–South line on the surface of the Earth where you are standing, or in the sky above your head. (2) **Greenwich Meridian –** The North–South line which passes through a particular telescope at the Old Royal Observatory at Greenwich. (2)

Meteor – Small boulder or particle of dust which enters the Earth's atmosphere at very high speed, heats up by friction with the atmosphere, and glows for a short period. They occur in showers, and usually burn themselves out in the upper atmosphere. (21)

Milky Way – The name given to the Galaxy to which we belong. (Intro.)

Monocular – One astronomical telescope fitted with inverting prisms. (17)

Nebula (pl. nebulae) – A glowing patch of gas within our own Galaxy. (17)

Nocturnal – A device for telling the time at night using the Plough and the Pole Star. (8)

Nova (pl. novae) – A star which explodes violently, causing it to increase in brightness over a few hours, and then gradually get fainter again over a matter of weeks. It is not a new star. **Supernova** – A massive star which explodes even more violently than a nova. (Before You Start)

Objective – Lens or mirror which collects the light from the object being viewed. (13)

Orrery – Model of Earth–Sun–Moon system which shows their relative motions. (22)

Penumbra (Umbra) – When a bright object (e.g. the Sun) casts a shadow of another body (e.g. the Moon) on a third body (e.g. the Earth), the area of the shadow can be divided into two parts; the area of partial shadow is called the penumbra, and the area of total shadow is called the umbra. (15)

Planet – A solid or semi-solid body orbiting the Sun. It is always nearly spherical in shape and it is only visible because it reflects the Sun's light. (Intro.)

Planisphere – A flat circular star map overlaid with a circular window. It can be used to show which stars are visible at any time of night on any night of the year. (10)

Pole of the sky – Point in the sky, very close to the North Star, around which the whole sky seems to turn. (6)

Prism – A thick glass triangle which can bend, reflect or split white light up into the colours of the rainbow. Used in a pair of binoculars or a monocular to turn an upside-down image the right way up. (17)

Quadrant – A quarter of a circle, formed by two radii at right angles to each other and part of the circumference of the circle. (3)

Radius (pl. radii) – The distance from the centre of the circle to the circumference. (1)

Real image – An image through which light actually passes and hence can be focussed on to a screen. (13)

Solar system – The 'family' of planets (of which the Earth is one), asteroids, moons, comets and other bodies and material which are held by gravity in orbit around our Sun. (Intro.)

Terminator – When the Moon is not full, only part of the side facing the earth is lit up by the Sun, and the terminator is the line dividing the light region from the dark region. (16)

Umbra – see Penumbra.

Virtual image – Image from which light appears to originate. Such an image cannot be focussed onto a screen, but it can be seen with the eye. (13)

Zenith – The highest point in the sky, vertically overhead, at any given place on Earth. (2)

APPENDIX 2 Equipment suppliers

Suppliers can be found all over the country, but here is a list of some of the main suppliers. In most cases equipment can be purchased by post.

Telescopes, finders, eyepieces, accessories and binoculars

Astro-bits, 211A Hightown Road, Luton LU2 0BZ.
Astro Books and Supplies, 47 Riddlesdown Avenue, Purley, Surrey CR2 1JL.
Astronomical Equipment Ltd, 45A Roundwood Lane, Harpenden, Herts.
Astro Instruments, 45 Derby Road, North End, Portsmouth, Hants.
Astro Systems Ltd, 58 Old Bedford Road, Luton LU2 7NX.
Bretmain Ltd, 99B Hamilton Road, Felixstowe, Suffolk.
Cambridge Astronomical Telescopes, Bucklebury House, The Green, Weston Colville, Cambs.
Charles Frank, PO Box, Carlton Park, Saxmundham, Suffolk, IP17 2NL.
Fullerscopes, 63 Farringdon Road, London EC1M 3JB.
The Planetarium, Armagh, Northern Ireland.

Photographic film for astrophotography

Bretmain Ltd, 99B Hamilton Road, Felixstowe, Suffolk.
Speedibrews, 54 Lovelace Drive, Pyrford, Woking, Surrey.

Monoculars

Scientific and Technical Ltd, Progress Road Trading Estate, Leigh-on-Sea, Essex.

Nocturnal

National Maritime Museum, Romney Road, Greenwich, London SE10.

APPENDIX 3 Astronomical societies

A The Junior Astronomical Society (JAS)

The best national society for a beginner to join since it caters specifically for beginners of all ages. Members can, if they wish, contribute actively to the observing sections which include: Solar; Lunar; Planetary; Astrophotographic; Meteor; Variable Star Groups.
The JAS publishes a very good quarterly magazine on popular astronomy and distributes circulars containing a great deal of useful information. For further details contact: The Secretary, JAS, 58 Vaughan Gardens, Ilford, Essex, IG1 3PD.

B The British Astronomical Association (BAA)

The association for the serious and devoted astronomer. Divided into following sections, each with its own Director: Sun; Moon; Mercury and Venus; Mars; Jupiter and Saturn; Comet; Meteor; Aurora; Variable Star; Instruments and Observing Method; Historical; Artificial Satellite.
The BAA publishes an annual handbook; a journal every two months; circulars giving information on topical events (e.g. novae, or comets); and occasional memoirs. Reduced subscription for members under 18 years of age. For details contact: Mrs F. A. Mobey, BAA, Burlington House, Piccadilly, London W1V 0NL.

C The Federation of Astronomical Societies

The Federation is a union of astronomical societies and groups working together for mutual benefit. Most societies in the country belong to the Federation, so for information on any in your area contact: Mr G. S. Pearce, Membership Secretary, 1 Valletort Cottages, Millbridge, Plymouth PL1 5PU.
The Federation publishes an annual *Handbook for Astronomical Societies*, containing some excellent articles on astronomy, list of astronomical societies in Great Britain, and an extensive list of equipment suppliers. Contact: Mr B. Jones, Publications Secretary, 'Alcyone', 28 High House Avenue, Bradford, W. Yorks, BD2 4ER.

D The Royal Astronomical Society

This Society has existed for over 150 years, and is mainly for professional astronomers, although amateurs are not excluded. Address: Burlington House, Piccadilly, London W1.

E The Association for Astronomy Education

This association has only just been founded. Its main aim is to promote astronomy education throughout the whole of the educational system in the United Kingdom, from school to university. It is open to all who wish to further this main aim. Further particulars from: Percy Seymour, William Day Planetarium, Plymouth Polytechnic, Drake Circus, Plymouth PL4 8AA.

APPENDIX 4 Book list

A General books

The Guinness Book of Astronomy, Facts and Feats by Patrick Moore (Guinness, 1979). This book contains not merely astronomical records, but also a large variety of facts relating to all aspects of astronomy. It is really a reference book, rather than a book to read from cover to cover.

Heavens Above by H. Cooper & T. Murtagh (Watts & Yorkshire Television). Written to accompany the Yorkshire TV programme of the same name, it is a good introduction to astronomy. Very up to date.

B Reference books

Key Definitions in Astronomy by J. Mitton (Miller, 1980). An extensive glossary of astronomical terms. Concise, easy to understand.

Astronomy Data Book by J. Hedley Robinson and J. Muirden (David & Charles, 1979). Systematic reference book on all aspects of astronomy from telescopes to galaxies. Also contains a good map of the Moon.

C Sundials

Sundials: How to Know, Use and Make Them by R. N. & M. W. Mayall (Sky Publishing Corporation, 1973). A thorough, yet readable and easily understood book covering all important aspects of the subject.

D Atlases or books containing star maps

What Star is That? by P. L. Brown (Viking Press, 1971). Systematic survey of the constellations and their origins; there are also notes on the stars within each constellation.

A Primer for Star-Gazers by H. M. Neely (Harper and Row, 1970). Mainly intended for those who are not seeking to become amateur astronomers but would nevertheless like to find their way around the sky.

Norton's Star Atlas and Reference Handbook by A. P. Norton (Sky Publishing Corporation, 1973). A must for any serious amateur. Not only contains detailed annotation maps of all sections of the sky, but also is crammed with other useful information.

E Information on positions of the planets

Monthly notes of the night sky are published in the following newspapers: *The Times, The Guardian, The Daily Telegraph, The Scotsman. The Times* also publishes an annual on The Night Sky for each year.

Sky and Telescope is a monthly magazine, published in America, that covers all aspects of astronomy. Also contains the planetary positions for each month. Obtainable from The Bookshop, The Planetarium, Armagh, N. Ireland.

F Binoculars and telescopes

Astronomy with Binoculars by J. Muirden (Faber and Faber Ltd, 1976). An excellent book full of useful tips and information on the wonders of the universe that can be revealed with an ordinary pair of binoculars.

Exploring the Moon through Binoculars by E. H. Charrington (McGraw Hill Book Co., 1969). Another good book on the use of binoculars: this one of course concentrates on the Moon.

Moon Map published by George Philip Printers Ltd, London. A detailed map of the Moon which can be very useful if you want to spend some time studying the Moon but do not wish to purchase a lunar atlas.

Make Your Own Telescope by R. Spry (Sidgwick and Jackson Ltd, 1978). Very straightforward and practical little book written by someone who has made some of Patrick Moore's telescopes.

Telescope Making, quarterly magazine devoted entirely to telescope making. Issues 4 and 5 have information on Dobsonian Telescopes of different sizes. Obtainable from Telescope Making Circulation Dept, Astromedia Corporation, PO Box 92788, Milwaukee, WI 53202, USA.

The Handbook of Astronomical Societies, published annually by Federation of Astronomical Societies (see Appendix 3). This publication often contains useful information on the making of telescopes. The 1981 edition contained details on how to make a 6 in. Dobsonian Telescope.

G Astrophotography

Astrophotography with Your Camera, Kodak Publication No. AC–20. A useful little pamphlet obtainable from Consumer Markets Division, Kodak, Rochester, New York, NY 14650, USA.

Stargazing with Telescope and Camera by G. T. Keene (Chilton Book Co., Philadelphia, 1967). A more extensive treatment of astrophotography. Useful if you want to concentrate on this particular topic.

APPENDIX 5 Apparent motions of planets in the night sky

Project 12 looked at how planets move against the background stars. They move at different speeds: sometimes they move from West to East against the stars, at other times they move from East to West. Their movements seem irregular, but this can be explained by the movement of Earth around the Sun combined with the motions of the planets themselves.

All planets, including the Earth, are moving in the same direction around the Sun, but the planets further from the Sun move more slowly (see the Table left).

Mercury and Venus are nearer the Sun than is the Earth; all the other planets are further out. Figs. A5.1 and A5.2 on page 68 show relative positions of Sun/Mercury/Earth and Sun/Earth/Jupiter.

Mercury moves faster than the Earth, therefore from the point of view of the Earth it will change its position rapidly in the sky. As the Earth moves through positions 1–9 on fig. A5.1, Mercury almost completes one orbit. The straight lines represent lines of sight from the Earth as Mercury makes its orbit, and as you can see Mercury appears to make loops in the sky.

As the Earth moves through points 1–11 in fig. A5.2, Jupiter, a slow-moving planet, covers only a small part of its orbit. The Earth's fast-changing point of view makes it appear that Jupiter moves in a loop against the background stars.

Planet	Distance from Sun	Time taken to orbit Sun
Mercury	57.9×10^6 km	88 Earth days
Venus	108.2×10^6 km	224 Earth days
Earth	149.6×10^6 km	$365\frac{1}{4}$ Earth days
Mars	227.9×10^6 km	687 Earth days
Jupiter	778.3×10^6 km	11.8 Earth years
Saturn	1427.0×10^6 km	29.45 Earth years
Uranus	2869.6×10^6 km	84 Earth years
Neptune	4496.6×10^6 km	164.8 Earth years
Pluto	5900×10^6 km	248.7 Earth years

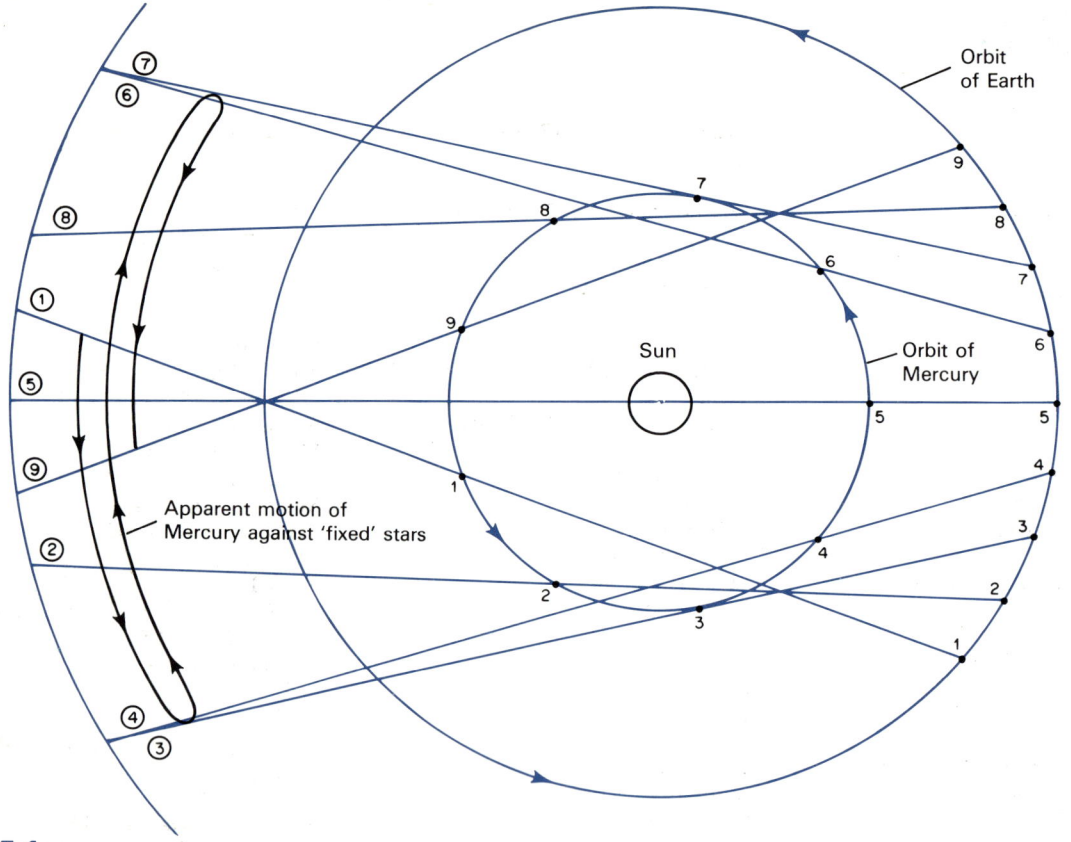

Fig. A5.1

Sun

Orbit of Earth

Orbit of Mercury

Apparent motion of Mercury against 'fixed' stars

(Distances and orbits are not exact)

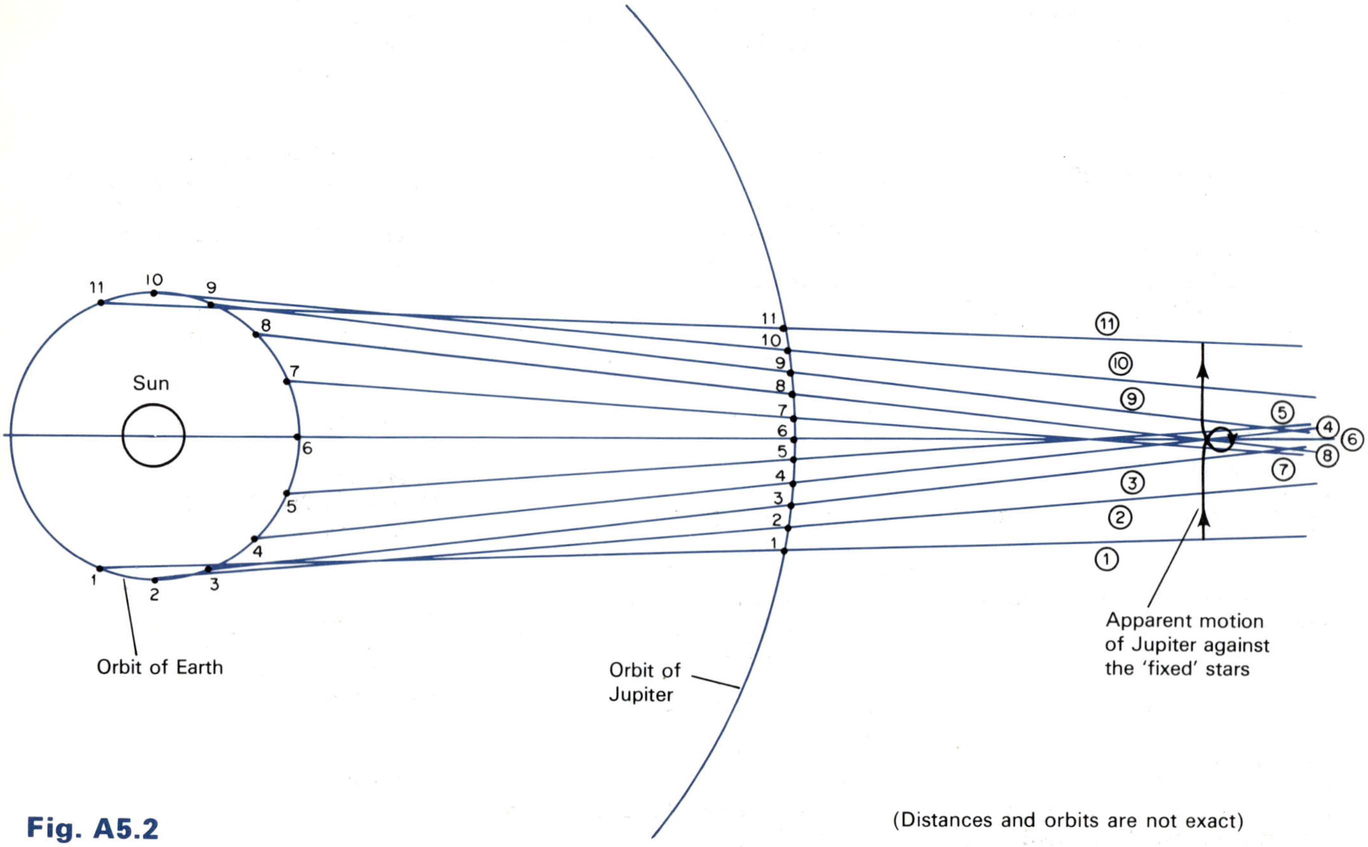

Fig. A5.2

Sun

Orbit of Earth

Orbit of Jupiter

Apparent motion of Jupiter against the 'fixed' stars

(Distances and orbits are not exact)

INDEX

SUMMER CONSTELLATIONS

DRACO

γ   β

Deneb

o

CYGNUS

LYRA

ε

Vega

β

M57

β

M92

M13

HERCULES

BOOTES

CORONA
BOREALIS

α

β

VULPECULA

M27

SAGITTA

Solar Apex

α

α

SERPENS

α

DELPHINUS

Altair

EQUULEUS

AQUILA

SERPENS

OPHIUCHUS

M5

β

M11

SCUTUM

η

LIBRA

α

CAPRICORNUS

M22

M8

× Centre of Galaxy

SCORPIUS

Antares

σ

SAGITTARIUS

M7

MICROSCOPIUM

ε

λ

CORONA
AUST.

TELESCOPIUM

LUPUS

NORMA

A R A

INDUS

SPRING CONSTELLATIONS

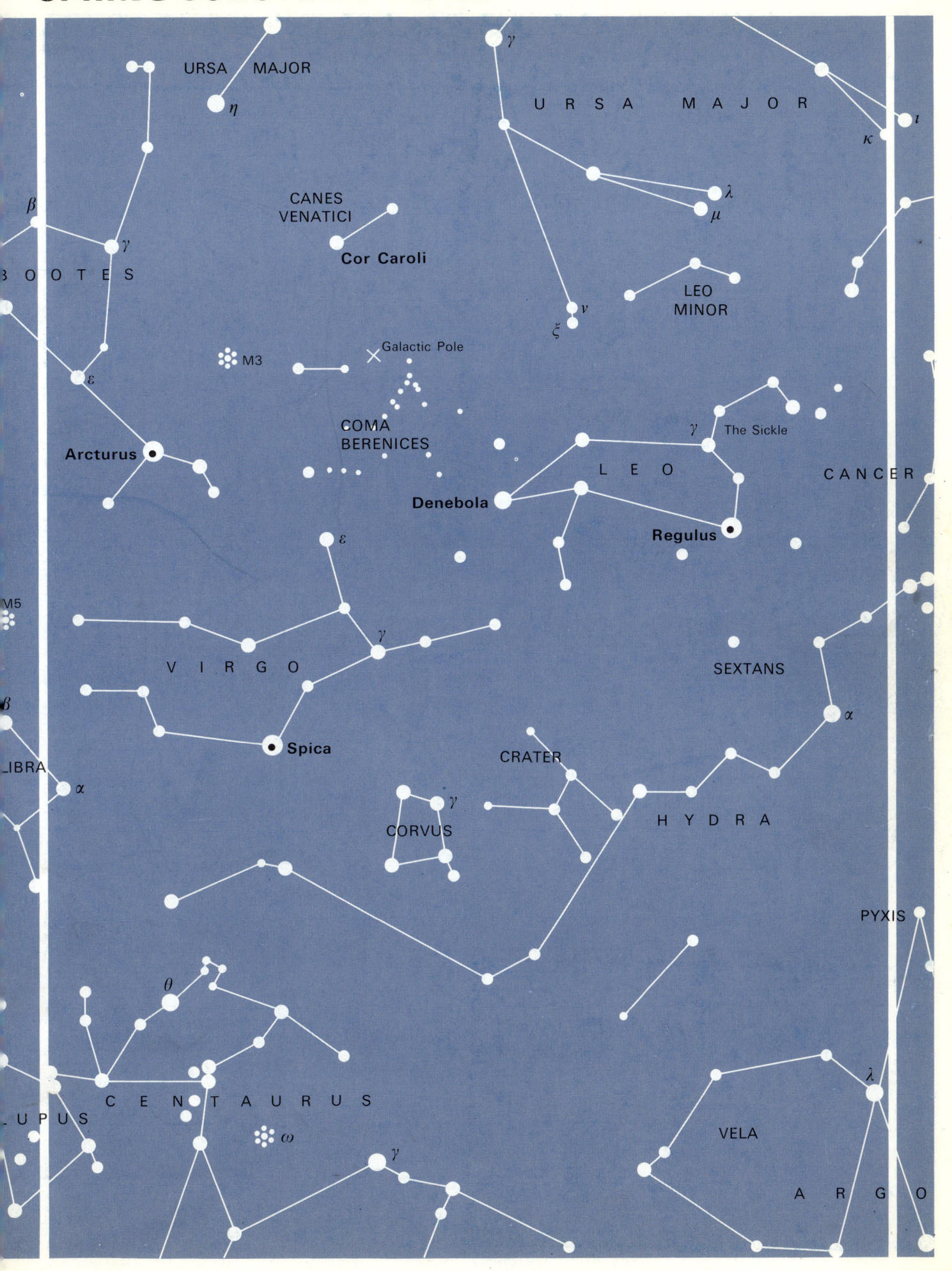

URSA MAJOR

η

URSA MAJOR

ι

κ

λ

μ

CANES
VENATICI

Cor Caroli

ν

ξ

LEO
MINOR

β

γ

BOOTES

ε

M3

Galactic Pole

COMA
BERENICES

γ

The Sickle

LEO

CANCER

Arcturus

Denebola

Regulus

ε

M5

ε

γ

VIRGO

SEXTANS

α

β

LIBRA

α

Spica

CRATER

HYDRA

γ

CORVUS

PYXIS

θ

λ

CENTAURUS

LUPUS

ω

VELA

γ

ARGO